THE NORTHERN ELEMENT
IN ENGLISH LITERATURE

THE NORTHERN ELEMENT
IN ENGLISH LITERATURE

BY

SIR WILLIAM CRAIGIE

Professor of English in the University of Chicago

TORONTO
THE UNIVERSITY OF TORONTO PRESS
1933

THE ALEXANDER LECTURES IN ENGLISH

AT

THE UNIVERSITY OF TORONTO

1931

Lecture I

IN spite of its place on the map, England has from the beginning produced a literature in which the North has a very slender share until quite recent times. Its models and its subjects have come to it mainly from the South—from actual contact with more southern countries, or from familiarity with their literatures throughout the centuries. To realize the truth of this, it is only necessary to pass in rapid review the great names of English literature and note the direction in which their works lead our thoughts. Take the great poets:—Chaucer with his *Canterbury Tales*, his *Troilus*, or his *House of Fame*; Gower with his *Confessio Amantis*; Lydgate with his *Siege of Thebes*, his *Troy Book*, or his *Falls of Princes*; the poetry of Surrey and Wyatt, of Spencer and Milton, of Dryden and Pope, of Byron and Browning. Scan the works of the dramatists, from the unknown authors of the mystery plays down through Shakespeare and the other Elizabethans, Beaumont and Fletcher, Dryden, Goldsmith, Sheridan, and practically all the modern playwrights of any note. Turn over the leaves of the great prose-writers from Malory, Elyot, and More, through Hooker, Hobbes, Bacon, Milton, Locke, Addison, Steele, *etc.*, down to our own days. The

result will in each case be the same; if the North
comes in at all, it is by way of exception or accident,
and not as a vital theme or inspiration. Even the
addition of Scottish authors to the ranks of those
who wrote in English did not have the effect which
might have been expected. Drummond of Hawthornden and the Earl of Stirling are northern
only by birth and residence, and the same is true
of David Hume, Henry Mackenzie, Dr. Hugh
Blair, and many more.

Another test may be applied with the same
effect. In the *Oxford Book of English Verse*, down
to the end of the sixteenth century, there is no
passage from any English author that either relates
to, or comes out of, the North, and of fourteen
pieces from the older Scottish poets not one has
any distinctive northern features. It is also
significant that when genuine northern verse
makes its first appearance in this collection, it does
so in a series of ballads and songs which stand out
in strong contrast to the classical English verse on
the pages which precede and follow. That the
contrast is so obvious is a proof that the North has
a voice of its own, and that the absence of it
throughout the greater part of English literature
must be due to special causes.

It may be objected that this review ignores the
fact that much of English literature has to do with
England itself. This is true, but the England of

the great writers we have named is not England of the rugged northern fells, of the bare northern moors, of the rushing mountain torrents, and the lonely tarns. It is England of the fertile fields and grassy meadows, of the blossomed hedgerows and the leafy copses, of the still pools and the placid, winding streams. It is England of the sunny southern aspect, "this other Eden, demy-paradise . . ,This precious stone, set in the silver sea". Even if stern truth forces the writer to dwell upon the less attractive aspects of nature, the cold of winter, the rains and floods of unkindly seasons, it is still the southern half of England that is present to his mind. The *Vision of Piers Plowman* or the *Eclogues* of Barclay show that there was no need to go to the North for the darker shades of English weather, and its depressing effects upon English rural life.

So careful, through many centuries, are English writers to avoid all mention of the North that one suspects they must have regarded it (if they thought of it at all) with the same aversion as their nearest kinsmen on the Continent, the Frisians, who gave it the significant name of *de grime herne*— "the grim corner" of the world, or the old Scandinavians who expressed in alliterative phrase their belief that "netherward and northward lies the way to Hell".

When we consider the matter more closely, it is, after all, obvious that there are good reasons why English literature should all along have had that inclination to the South, as steadfast almost as the needle to the pole. Except in its very earliest period, of which we really know very little, even Anglo-Saxon literature, in verse as well as in prose, was largely based on Latin learning. Over against the verse that deals with native legends—the *Beowulf* and the fragments of other heroic poems—and two or three historical pieces, we have the *Genesis*, *Exodus*, and *Daniel*, the *Andreas*, *Juliana*, and *Elene*, the *Phœnix*, the *Metres* of Boethius, and more besides, all directly drawn from Latin originals, and all, with the exception of the two poems on Saint Guthlac, dealing with southern or oriental themes. Whether these can be said to contain any northern elements in the treatment of the subjects we shall consider later. With rare exceptions, such as the greater portion of the *Chronicle*, Anglo-Saxon prose is even more a direct result of southern influence. It was only because the knowledge of Latin had declined during the ninth century that Alfred bent his energies to replace it by a literature of translation, and no later Anglo-Saxon writer had any other ideal or model before him.

Even Middle English literature carries on the same tradition, unaffected by the Scandinavian settlements in the North of England or the Scandinavian origin of the Norman conquerors. The only difference is that the southern influence now comes from nearer at hand, that it is of French, rather than of Latin, origin. It is unnecessary to illustrate this by any review of the literature as a whole. To take a single field, that in which there would naturally be the greatest freedom in geographical range—the romances—it requires only a brief survey of these to see how dependent they are on French originals or models. This is true even of those which are connected with English soil—*Bevis of Hampton*, *Guy of Warwick*, or *Richard Coeur-de-lion*. Exceptionally, the romance of *Havelok* tells a tale which connects England and Denmark, but this also has a French original, and the English version displays no independent knowledge of Danish affairs. The most thoroughly English type of romance—the alliterative—is no less dependent on French and even Latin originals than the rhyming. Witness the titles of the *Wars of Alexander*, the *Destruction of Troy*, the *Morte Arthure*, and *William of Palerne*. With themes like these it will be all the more significant if we can detect any qualities which may fairly be attributed to the northern origin or traditions of their authors. How heavy the balance against the North in romance and kindred subjects was may also be realized from the fact that of forty-five popular tales mentioned in the *Complaint of Scotland* in 1549 only six or seven are on northern subjects.

This southern influence was all the more powerful because there was so little from the other quarter that could be set against it. The northern lands, coming late into the number of civilized nations, had developed no literary culture comparable to that of the South. So far as they had any interest in such culture, they were learners and not teachers. Books, which are the natural medium by which a learned literature is disseminated, went north, and not south, unless (like the works of Bede or Aldhelm) they were reflexes of the learning which had already come from the South. With no philosophy of its own, no theology, no science or speculation, no ancient history, the North had nothing to offer in exchange except a highly-developed art of poetry and story-telling, and neither of these availed anything, since the language, whether Irish or Old Norse, was too hard to be understood without much effort, and was not a subject of regular study as Latin was.

In the circumstances, the preponderating southern influence could only have been effectively counteracted if the English had felt and cultivated an interest in themselves and their surroundings, their legends and history, their relations to the countries and peoples around them, and had made these a dominant note in their literature. It was by a lively interest in such things that the Icelanders, in far less favourable circumstances, were able to produce a literature to which no other northern country presents a parallel. Not that the Icelanders were ignorant of southern culture; they read and translated extensively from both Latin and French, but they valued their own poetry so highly, they were so eager to record their own legend and history and that of all the countries with which they had natural connections, that the literature they produced from the tenth to the thirteenth centuries forms the most striking contrast to that of England during the same period. The Anglo-Saxon seems to have been strangely lacking in the gift of telling a tale at first hand and in his own language; such examples as do occur are rare and brief. A significant instance of how opportunities for doing so could be missed is found in the account of St. Edmund in East Anglia, whose tale was told by his sword-bearer to King Athelstan, in the hearing of Dunstan, when the sword-bearer was an old man and Dunstan still a youth. Later on Dunstan retold it to Abbo of Fleury, while the latter was on a visit to him. The foreigner recognized the interest of the tale and wrote it down in Latin. Then Ælfric came along, took the Latin account, and translated it into Anglo-Saxon. It apparently never occurred to

Dunstan or to anyone else to write down the story in the sword-bearer's own language, as an Icelander would have done.

This complete difference in mental attitude, which sufficiently accounts for the absence of the North from Anglo-Saxon literature, could be illustrated by numerous examples, but one will suffice. The account of the Battle of Stamford Bridge in the *Anglo-Saxon Chronicle* is brief and bald, a mere record of the principal details without life or colour, or even any appreciation of the importance of the event. To turn from this to the pages of the *Saga of Harald hardrádi,* and see how the Icelandic writer deals with the same theme, brings out at once the essential difference between the two literatures. Although the English account is contemporary with the battle, and the Icelandic, in its written form, is a century and a half later, the saga-writer achieves a vivid picture of the whole series of events from the landing of King Harald—his unexpected meeting with the English army, the verses he made on that occasion, the dramatic interview between the English king and Earl Tosti, the battle itself, and the flight of the Norwegians, even to the incident of the one who met the English carter and killed him for the sake of his cloak. To bring out the difference clearly, it will suffice to compare the full account as given in the *Chronicle* with a single passage of the saga.

In the meantime [says the chronicler] Harald the English King came with all his army to Tadworth, and
there drew up his forces, and then on the Monday went
out through York. Harald, the King of Norway, and
Earl Tostig and their army had gone from their ships
beyond York to Stamford Bridge, because they had
been assured that hostages from all the shires would be
brought to them there. Then Harald the English King
came upon them unawares beyond the bridge, and they
there joined battle, and were fighting strenuously for a
long time during the day. There Harald, the King of
Norway, was slain, and Earl Tostig, and unnumbered
others with them, both of Northmen and English, and
the Northmen fled from the English.

A much later hand adds a more vivid detail:

There was one of the Norwegians who withstood the
English, so that they might not cross the bridge and
obtain the victory. One of the English shot at him
with an arrow, but it availed nothing. Then another
came under the bridge, and thrust him beneath his
mail coat. Then Harold the King came over the
bridge and his army with him.

How bare and colourless this is appears all the
more when it is contrasted with the saga-writer's
account of a single episode:

After that there rode forward twenty knights in front
of the array of the Northmen, and they were all clad
in mail, and so were their horses. Then one of the
knights said, "Is Earl Tosti in the host?" He answers,
"It is not to be denied that you may find him here."
Then the knight said, "King Harald your brother sends
you his greeting, and this message with it, that you
shall have terms of peace, and possession of all North-

umberland.   And rather than have you refuse to come
over to his side, he will give you a third of the kingdom."
Earl Tosti answered, "Now something else is offered
than contempt and hostility, as was the case last
autumn.   If this offer had been made then that is
made now, many a man would now be alive who will
never see his home again, and the rule of England's
King would stand in better state.   Now, if we accept
this offer, what will my brother offer to Harald the
king of the Northmen for his labours?"   The knight
answers, "The king has said something about what he
will grant him of England.   He shall have seven feet
of space, or so much the more as he is taller than other
men."   Then the earl said, "Go now and tell my
brother Harald to prepare for battle.   The Northmen
shall have another tale to tell than that Earl Tosti
left King Harald and joined his enemies when he was
to fight for the kingship of England.   Rather shall we
all take one counsel, to die here with honour, or win
England with victory."   Thereupon the knights rode
back again.

After that King Harald Sigurdson said to Earl
Tosti: "Who was that well-spoken man who talked
with you?"   The Earl answered, "That was King
Harald Godwinson himself."   Then said King Harald,
"Too long was I kept ignorant of this, for they were in
such a place before our host that my namesake would
not have been able to speak of any victory over us."
The earl answers: "We saw, sir, that so great a leader
acted unwarily, and it might have been as you say.
He came here because he wished to offer peace and
power to his brother.   I might then truly be called a
chief of a worse kind, if I lived to old age as the slayer
of my brother."   Then King Harald said to his men:

"This was a little man, lads, but he stood proudly in his stirrups."

It matters little whether all this is fact or fiction. If it is fact, no Anglo-Saxon writer thought it worth recording; and if it is fiction, it required the far North to invent it, recognizing that there was real dramatic propriety in the interview, whether it actually took place or not. However we take it, it illustrates as clearly as anything can the essential difference between the unimaginative South and the interested and inventive North, and shows how much English literature in its earlier days lost by the absence of that northern spirit.

Still more unfavourable for any manifestation of northern interests in older English literature was the lack of literary activity in the North of England itself. It has commonly been supposed that a considerable part of the Anglo-Saxon poetry which has come down to us is of Northumbrian origin, but this is by no means certain. Anglian no doubt it is, rather than Saxon, but the astonishment excited at Whitby by the very primitive verses of Cædmon might be advanced as an argument that good poetry was something rare in Northumbria, in the time of the Abbess Hild at least. There is only one piece of Anglo-Saxon poetry which can be localized, that on the *Battle of Maldon*, and that is definitely East Anglian. It has also been suggested

2

that the description of the home of Grendel and his mother in the *Beowulf* indicates a Northumbrian poet's endeavour to depict coast-scenery with which he was familiar. This is mere conjecture, as the nature of the place inhabited by the monsters may equally well have belonged to the original Scandinavian story.

Even if we grant the early Northumbrian poetry, however, there remains a period of several centuries down to the close of the thirteenth, during which the North of England is absolutely barren of anything in the way of a native literature. How remarkable this long silence is may be realized by remembering that the golden age of Icelandic poetry and prose was already past before Yorkshire and Northumberland became vocal in their native speech. Yet they could, if they had been so inclined, have had as much to tell, and of as varied interest, as the poets and historians in that remote island of the north Atlantic. It was not matter that they lacked, but the will or the ability to make use of it.

The neglect of the North in all this earlier English literature was made all the more possible by two or three important factors—by ignorance, indifference, or actual antipathy. This lack of knowledge or understanding, and the absence of any friendly feeling, applied not only to the remote North, to the Scandinavian countries, but to the

northern part of Britain itself. That knowledge
of early Scandinavian history and legend which is
so clearly manifested in the *Beowulf* had died out
before the descents of the Vikings began. King
Alfred's interest in the accounts of Norway and
of the Baltic given him by Ohthere and Wulfstan
cannot be regarded as typical; they were a valuable
supplement, based on first-hand information, to
the geography of Europe which he was translating
from the Latin of Orosius. During the long-drawn
period of the Norwegian and Danish invasions,
there is no sign that even the chronicler was
interested in the countries from which they came.
For several centuries these seem to have been little
more than mere names to the ordinary Englishman,
while Sweden was hardly known even by name.
When Robert of Gloucester has occasion to
mention the king of Sweden, he makes himself
intelligible to his readers by calling him "the King
of biside Danemark". Even as late as 1542,
Andrew Boorde, with all his pretensions to
knowledge, could still assure his readers that
Norway was "a great ilond", that "the countre is
wylde, and there be many rewde people". Of the
Icelanders, who in that very age had produced men
of action and intellect like the poet-bishop Jón
Arason, he has no hesitation in saying that they
are "beastly creatures, vnmannered and vntaughte.
They have no houses, but yet doth lye in caves,

al together lyke swyne. . .They be lyke the people
of the newe founde land named Calyco."[1]

While such statements could pass current, it
would be hopeless to expect the Scandinavian
North to play any part in English literature. The
ignorance and antipathy, however, like charity,
began at home, and was quite as strong in the
several parts of Britain in relation to those who
lived further north. The Saxon had frequent
occasion to regard the Anglian as an enemy rather
than an ally. The Anglian had equal reason to
dislike the Pict and the Scot. The Englishman of
a later date could see no good in anyone born north
of the Border, while the Lowland Scot with his
Anglian speech held as strong opinions regarding
all the inhabitants of the Highlands. On these
accounts, any references to the dwellers in the
North appearing in English literature down to a
late date, are likely to be derogatory. The
southern Englishman even disliked the speech of
the Northerner, and the remarks of Higden on this
point are amplified, evidently with thorough
approval, by his translator, John of Trevisa.

> All the language of the Northumbrians, and specially
> at York, is so sharp, slitting and frotting, and un-
> shapen, that we Southern may scarcely understand
> that language. I trow that is because they be nigh
> to strange men, and aliens that speak strangely, and

[1]Andrew Boorde, *Introduction of Knowledge* (Early English Text
Society), chap. vi, p. 141.

also because the Kings of England were always far from that country.[1]

The author of the *Owl and Nightingale*, with a low opinion of northern culture in respect of music, makes the owl taunt the nightingale with neglecting an obvious mission to set a better model in that quarter.

> Thou never singest in Ireland; thou never comest in Scotland. Why wilt thou not fare to Norway, and sing to men of Galloway? There are men that know little of any song that is beneath the sun. Why wilt thou not sing there to priests, and teach them of thy warbling, and show them by thy voice how angels sing in heaven?[2]

To be unable to speak elegantly, or to sing harmoniously, are no doubt serious defects, but there were worse charges which English writers had to bring against the Scots. The usual epithet applied to them by the chroniclers is "false", which, however, the Scots retorted with equal conviction of its justice. "Ware yet with the Scots, for they are full of guile", says Laurence

[1]Higden's *Polychronicon* (Rolls Series), vol. II. pp. 158-161.
[2]*The Owl and Nightingale*, pp. 907-916.
Thu neuer ne singest in Irlonde,
Ne thu ne cumest in Scotlonde,
Hwi nultu fare to Noreweie,
An singin men of Galaweie?
Thar beoth men that lutel kunne
Of songe that is bineothe the sunne.
Whi nultu thare preoste singe,
An teche of thine writelinge,
An wisi hom mid thire steuene
Hu engeles singeth ine heuene?

Minot, and couples the warning with the further charges of pride and poverty, which are repeated by later writers. Andrew Boorde, for example, in his brief account of Scotland, makes the Scot say of himself:

> I am a Scottish man, and have dissembled much,
> And in my promise I have not kept touch.

Admitting some of their good qualities, he yet finds them intolerable braggarts: "The people of the country be hardy men, and strong men, and well favoured, and good musicians, but of all nations they will face, crack, and boast themselves, their friends, and their country, above reason; for many will make strong lies." From his own experience, too, he had learned that they had no love for their English neighbours. "It is naturally given, or it is of a devilish disposition of a Scottish man, not to love nor favour an Englishman."[1]

Whoever has read the *Fortunes of Nigel* will remember how Richie Moniplies, thinking that he had an ignorant Southerner to deal with, tried to vaunt the Water of Leith and the Nor' Loch as compared with the Thames. Here, as usual, Scott is historically correct in crediting Richie with a weakness for which his countrymen were specially noted.

[1]Andrew Boorde, *Introduction of Knowledge*, chap. iv, pp. 135-137.

2

How, then, was it possible in the face of all this ignorance, indifference, or positive antipathy, for the voice of the North to make itself heard among the varied strains of English literature? That it has done so, and that it has spoken clearly and powerfully in later times, is plain enough, and the stages by which it has gained a hearing, and has been listened to with growing interest and admiration, will bear tracing in some detail. The process was at first a slow one, and only attained success when several converging causes at last came together, and enabled the voice to fall upon ears that had been gradually prepared to welcome it.

One of the factors was a growing interest in the various forms of English, and in the northern tongues. The enthusiasm for the older English poets, Chaucer, Gower, and Lydgate, which prevailed in the early part of the sixteenth century, made it more possible to understand and enjoy those northern writers who used their own dialect. Surrey evidently found no difficulty in reading Gawin Douglas's intensely Scottish translation of Virgil in manuscript, and the printer Copland must have reckoned on a body of English readers to buy the edition when he printed the whole of that work in 1554, without modifying the language towards an English standard. In the following century

William De L'Isle found this version of special
value to him for the help it gave with Anglo-Saxon,
the study of which (beginning in the sixteenth
century) steadily led English scholars to a wider
interest in the northern tongues—an interest which,
on the scholarly side, culminated in George Hickes's
stately tomes, the *Thesaurus Linguarum Sept-
entrionalium.*   All this helped to prepare the way
for understanding and appreciating the Scottish
dialect-poetry which began to attract notice shortly
after the opening of the eighteenth century.

These learned studies, of course, had little
effect on English literature of the sixteenth and
seventeenth centuries, which, for the most part,
adhered steadfastly to the standard laid down by
George Puttenham, if he was the author of the
Arte of English Poesie.   The author of that work
had no doubt of the unsuitability of the northern
tongue for use in poetry.

> Our maker at these dayes shall not follow Piers Plow-
> man, nor Gower, nor Lydgate nor yet Chaucer, for
> their language is now out of use with us.   Neither shall
> we take the terms of Northern men, such as they use
> in dayly talke, whether they be noblemen or gentlemen,
> or of their best clarkes, all is one matter; nor in effect
> any speech used beyond the river of Trent, though no
> man can deny that theirs is the purer English Saxon
> at this day, yet it is not so courtly nor so current as
> our Southern English is.[1]

[1][George Puttenham], *The Arte of English Poesie*, bk. III, chap. lv.

While such views were held by the critics, it is
not surprising that English writers made few
attempts to use the northern dialect either in verse
or prose. Bullein in his *Dialogue* of 1564 makes
one of the speakers a Northumbrian, but evidently
soon grew tired of trying to write the dialect, or
was afraid of wearying his readers with too much
of it. In *Albion's England* Warner brings in
"a simple Northerne man" to declaim against
monks and friars in a dozen stanzas of dialect,
obviously artificial. The dialect in Spenser's
Shepherd's Calendar of 1579 is midland and southern in the main, but contains a few northern words
and forms which are explained by the commentator,
sometimes with an indication of their origin.
"The Gate", he says is "the Gote. Northernly
spoken to turn o into a." In the phrase " 'Wae is
me', *wae* is 'woe Northernly'. Similarly 'heame'
for 'home', after the northern pronouncing."
Others which he explains without such comments,
are "what gars thee greete" (causeth the weep and
complain), "thou kenst" (knowest), "all the kirke
(church) pillours", "warke" (work), "gange" (goe),
"mirke" (obscure), "war" (worse). These are but
modest lessons in northern speech, but they are
significant of a desire to introduce a northern local
colour into pastoral poetry, which had hitherto
been definitely southern in character.

These examples did not incite many to follow

them. Green in his *James IV* (which has no connection with Scotland beyond the misleading title) makes one of his characters, Bohan, speak a mixture of Scottish and northern English, but Shakespeare was too wise to attempt anything of the kind in *Macbeth*, nor did the author of the short *Yorkshire Tragedy* try to introduce any local touches in his dialogue. So far from the North invading English literature through the medium of language, the current flowed altogether in the other direction.

Another important factor was an increasing knowledge of the history of Scotland and the northern lands, made possible by the appearance of a series of works during the sixteenth and seventeenth centuries. The history of Scotland had, indeed, been written at length by John of Fordun and his continuator Walter Bower, by Andrew of Wyntoun, by the compiler of the *Book of Pluscarden*, and others, but these works, produced before the invention of printing, were little known outside the country of their origin. Circumstances had altered when John Major, Hector Boece, George Buchanan, and Bishop Leslie successively recounted both the fabulous and the genuine lives of Scottish kings, and the events of Scottish history, in fluent Latin and in printed volumes. These gave ample opportunity to English scholars to make themselves acquainted with interesting tales and dramatic incidents previously unknown to them, and to arouse an interest in Scotland's past similar to that which they already felt for their own country. When Holinshed's chronicle of England was augmented by a chronicle of Scotland, drawn from the work of Hector Boece, all this new matter became accessible to the ordinary English reader. Some had no doubt read it in the Scottish translation by John Bellenden, of which William Harrison made use to save himself the trouble of translating from Boece's Latin. In introducing his version of the *Description of Scotland* he says:

> I have chose rather, onlie with the loss of three or four days, to translate Hector out of the Scottish (a tongue very like unto ours) than with more expense of time to devise a new, or follow the Latin copy which is more large and copious. How excellently, if you consider the art, Boetius hath penned it, and the rest of his historie, in Latin, the skilful are not ignorant; but how profitably and compendiously John Bellenden, archdeacon of Murray, his interpreter, hath turned him from the Latin into the Scottish tongue, there are very few Englishmen that know, because we want the books.[1]

From Holinshed, it is needless to say, Shakespeare took the story of *Macbeth*, which had long before been told in Scottish verse by Andrew of Wyntoun, and later by William Stewart in his

[1]William Harrison, *The Description of Scotland*, in Holinshed's *Chronicle* (ed. 1587).

metrical translation of Boece's history.   Thus
again, as in the days of Ælfric, a tale of native
origin had to pass through Latin before receiving
due recognition in English.

In addition to the histories, the course of
political events after the Union of the Crowns
naturally attracted more attention to Scotland.
The campaigns of Cromwell and Monk, the careers
of Montrose and Claverhouse, the risings of 1715
and 1745, all contributed to bring the North more
prominently into notice and to rouse an interest
which was not confined to the events of the day.
If the Highlands still remained largely an unknown
country supposedly peopled by a wild and half
savage race, the Lowlands were coming to be
understood, and literary intercourse between North
and South was steadily increasing, opening up
possibilities of new influences from the northern
side.

The Scandinavian North, too, was emerging
from the mists which had so long obscured it.   The
poetry and prose of Iceland, unknown to the outer
world so long as they remained in their original
form, began to break through the barriers of
language by being translated into Latin, or by
supplying matter for learned works on northern
history and antiquities. The writings of the
Swedish bishops, Petrus and Olaus Magnus, of the
learned Icelander, Arngrímur Jónsson, of the

Danish antiquaries, Worm and Bartholin, of
Thormôdur Torfason (latinized as Torfæus), together with editions of various sagas accompanied
by Latin translations, were all eagerly received by
those whose interest had been awakened in the
early history and literature of the North.   An echo
of these early writers still lingers in the lines with
which Scott concluded his *Harold the Dauntless* in
1817:

> I will not borrow,
> To try thy patience more, one anecdote
> From Bartholine, or Peringskiöld, or Snorro.

This is a subject which has already been worked
out in detail,[1] and it is unnecessary to go minutely
into it here.   It is sufficient to realize that the
opportunities for northern studies were not only
steadily increasing during the seventeenth and
eighteenth centuries, but that the results of these
studies were becoming more and more familiar
to English readers.

The effect on English literature of this line of
interest, however, is not noticeable until after the
middle of the eighteenth century, for Shakespeare's
Hamlet, ultimately drawn from the Danish history
of Saxo Grammaticus (again a Latin medium),
came in by accident and by another channel.
The significant dates in this connection are 1763,

[1] F. E. Farley, *Scandinavian Influences in the English Romantic
Movement* (1903), and C. H. Nordby, *The Influence of Old Norse Literature upon English Literature* (1901).

when Bishop Percy brought out anonymously his *Five Pieces of Runic Poetry*, "translated from the Icelandic language", and 1768, when the *Fatal Sisters* and the *Descent of Odin* appeared among the poems of Gray.

To the growing knowledge of northern history and antiquities there was added a clearer idea of the North itself, both in Britain and Scandinavia. The descriptions of Scotland by Boece (ultimately finding its way into Holinshed), Buchanan, and Leslie, were supplemented by later works in English, a number of which were written in a lively and readable style. Martin's *Late Voyage to St. Kilda, the remotest of all the Hebrides*, published in 1698, gives an interesting account of the inhabitants of that island, living in primitive "innocence and simplicity", among the vast flocks of solan geese and other sea-fowl. Captain Edward Burt's *Letters from the North*, written about 1730 and printed in 1754, gave "an account of the Highlands, with the Customs and Manners of the Highlanders", which (as the title page states) was "interspersed with Facts and Circumstances entirely new to the Generality of the People in England, and little known in the Southern Parts of Scotland". Thomas Pennant's *Tours in Scotland* in 1769 and 1772 furnished English readers with a mass of accurate information on topographical and historical matters, combined with interesting accounts of Scottish customs and beliefs, while those of Boswell and Johnson had the added interest of association with one of the great literary figures of the day. A survey of such works shows very clearly how the way was being steadily and effectively prepared for the triumphant advent of Scotland in literature which came with the early years of the nineteenth century.

Blank ignorance, or absurd fancies, regarding the northern lands were also being dissipated by more accurate information. The description of the Færöes by the Danish clergyman, Lucas Debes, appeared in English in 1676, and was preceded (in 1674) by Scheffer's account of Lapland. English versions of Pontoppidan's *Natural History of Norway*, and Horrebow's *Natural History of Iceland*, published in 1755 and 1758 respectively, and of Von Troil's *Letters on Iceland*, appearing in 1780, came opportunely to satisfy or to stimulate the curiosity of those who were becoming interested in northern studies. After 1800 there was abundant material in English for anyone who cared to pursue the subject.

By the steady multiplication of such aids, English scholars and English readers were attaining more and more to some knowledge of a whole world that had hitherto lain out of their ken. Attention which previously had been either self-centred, or directed towards the South, was now being gradually turned towards the North, and with the increasing knowledge of the countries and their inhabitants, some faint ideas were being introduced of literature and literary themes, hitherto unsuspected or ignored. It was long before these ideas found expression, for even the northern contributors to English literature, the Scottish writers of the seventeenth and eighteenth centuries, showed no more readiness to use these new themes than did their English contemporaries. Sir Robert Aytoun, Sir William Alexander, Drummond of Hawthornden, hold whatever rank they may have in English literature in virtue of work which has no Scottish element in it. The same is true, for the most part, of those Scots of the eighteenth century who attained any position in the world of English letters—Thomson, Hume, Smollett, Blair, or Mackenzie. John Home obtained some reputation for his tragedy of *Douglas*, but except for the few lines in the second act, beginning with the well-known words:

My name is Norval; on the Grampian hills
My father feeds his flocks,

there is really less of Scotland in *Douglas* than there is in *Macbeth*. The titles of Home's other tragedies are significant enough—*Agis*, *Alfred*, *Alonzo*, the *Siege of Aquileia*, the *Fatal Discovery*. When Home, during a visit to London, inspired Collins to write his *Ode on the Popular Super-*

stitions of the Highlands in Scotland, he aided a true-born Englishman to display more of the spirit of the North than he had done himself. Smollett did, however, give some attention to his native country in *Humphrey Clinker*, which has a certain significance on that account.

3

From all this it is clear that little interest in, or knowledge of, the North is to be expected from anything written in standard English before the eighteenth century. Literature, however, was not confined to the southern areas in which that standard language was formed and from which it subsequently spread. There was also a northern literature in the Middle English period, and when that ceased on English ground, it continued to flourish north of the Border for some time, without losing the name of English and assuming that of Scottish. Even to an ardent (some will say, an intolerant) patriot like Blind Harry, the natural tongue of a Scot was still "Inglis", and, inconsistently enough, it is Gavin Douglas whom we find first insisting on calling his language "Scottis", while he went further than any other poet of his time in interlarding it with southern English forms which he learned from Chaucer.

If we are to discover what northern traces there are in English literature, it will obviously be of

3

use to examine this northern literature, so far as it deals with local or native themes, and see what its leading features are. We may safely pass over most of what it has in common with the South in the way of literary material; outside of the difference in dialect it would be difficult, and perfectly arbitrary, to attempt to discover differences in spirit or in the manner of treating a subject. There are, however, some points in which even here a distinction may be justifiably drawn.

In the choice of subjects, the northern English writers of the fourteenth century—the period during which they were most active and independent—are distinctly disappointing. They have left us copious specimens of their industry both in prose and verse, but they rarely touch a theme which has any local connection. They will discourse on any matter of history that concerns the ancient Jews or Greeks, the early Christians, or the Arthurian legend, on all manner of saints or heroes of romance, on practical or mystical religion, but they carefully avoid anything about which they could have written with first-hand knowledge. In this respect they fully maintain the Anglo-Saxon literary tradition; whatever they write has a written prototype which is more or less closely followed. If there are any exceptions to this, they are in subjects which do not help our quest, like the religious meditations of Rolle of Hampole.

Even when a northern theme is selected for versifying, such as the legend of Saint Cuthbert, the rule of a literary original still holds, and the fresh treatment of the subject tells us nothing new.

To the north of the Border we are on much more promising ground. Scottish literature begins with a work of a national character, the *Bruce* of John Barbour, which by its subject is necessarily connected with the North, and involves an anti-pathy to the South, which is strongly expressed in certain passages. The *Bruce* is important because of its popularity down to the eighteenth century; its effect on later literature is most clearly seen in Scott's *Lord of the Isles*. The later books of the *Original Chronicle* of Andrew of Wyntoun, and the anonymous author whose work he incorporated, are of value, not for any poetic merit, but for some of the incidents they relate. Late in the fifteenth century the *Buke of the Howlat*, in the main a retelling of the fable of the owl in borrowed plumes, is important for two passages. One of these is typical of the Scottish contempt for the Irish bard; the other is an eloquent account of the exploits and death of Douglas in fighting against the Saracens while he carried with him the heart of Bruce.

In the *Wallace* of Blind Harry both subject and sentiment are thoroughly national, and a careful study of the poem brings out clearly examples of some of the distinctive features of northern poetry.

Nearly forty years ago I endeavoured to prove at length that Blind Harry (whatever his defects as a historian might be) was in every way a better poet than Barbour. I am still of that opinion, and am equally certain that he has far more of the northern spirit than the archdeacon.

The greatest of the old Scottish poets, Henryson, Dunbar, and Douglas, have unfortunately little that is definitely northern in their work. Henryson's version of *Aesop's Fables*, his *Orpheus and Eurydice*, his *Testament of Cresseid*, Douglas's *Palace of Honour* and translation of the *Aeneid*, are as southern in origin as they can well be. There is more of a local nature in Dunbar's verse, but little of it can be reckoned among his best work, with the exception of the *Lament for the Makaris*. The *Flyting*, however, contains an interesting attack upon Gaelic and Highlanders, countered by Kennedy's defence. Even Douglas's prologues rarely touch on subjects of a northern interest, although the description of winter in that to the seventh book distinctly suggests its place of origin.

Greatly inferior as a poet to any of these, Sir David Lyndsay is far more national both in his subjects and in his manner of handling them. For both of these reasons his works continued to be widely read in Scotland when those of his greater predecessors were little known. Pinkerton,

who deplored the fact, bears testimony to the
popularity of Lyndsay towards the close of the
eighteenth century.   His remarks on that head are
worth quoting, as they also exhibit very clearly the
attitude of the eighteenth century purist towards
the survival of the dialects.

> Perhaps some may say that the Scots themselves wish
> to abolish their dialect totally, and substitute the
> English; why then attempt to preserve the Scotish
> language? Let me answer that none can more
> sincerely wish a total extinction of the Scotish collo-
> quial dialect than I do, for there are few modern
> Scoticisms which are not barbarisms. . . .
>
>   Yet, I believe no man of either kingdom would wish
> the extinction of the Scotish dialect in poetry . . . but
> it were to be wished that it should be regarded only
> as an ancient and poetical language, and nothing can
> take it so much out of the hands of the vulgar as a
> rigid preservation of the old spelling.   Were there no
> Scotish books that the common people in Scotland
> could read, their knowledge of the English would
> increase very rapidly.   But while they are enraptured
> with Barbour's History of Bruce, Blind Harry's Life of
> Wallace, and the works of Sir David Lindsay, books to
> be found in modern spelling at this day in almost every
> cottage in Scotland, their old dialect will maintain its
> ground.   Were the books to be published only in their
> original orthography not one in a hundred of the
> peasantry could read them, and of course, they would
> be forced to read English.[1]

[1] J. Pinkerton, *Ancient Scottish Poems* (1786), preface, pp. xvii-xviii.

After Lyndsay, it is unnecessary to consider any other Scottish poet of the sixteenth century in the hope of getting further light upon northern characteristics, although Sempill and Sir Richard Maitland may supply good matter for shrewd notes on the various types of Scottish character during those troubled times. In place of these, it will be much more instructive, because less open to the suspicion of outward influence, to turn to the more popular literature of the late sixteenth and the seventeenth century—the ballads and songs, and the nameless pieces which are to be classed with these rather than with the work of the conventional poets. Even if we eliminate the ballads which deal with themes that are known outside of Scotland, there remain enough that bear in their very titles the stamp of their origin—the *Battles of Otterbourne* or *Harlaw*, the *Raid of the Reidswire*, the *Lads of Wamphray*, *Jamie Telfer of the Fair Dodheid*, the *Fire of Frendraucht*, the *Coble of Cargill*, the *Bonny House of Airlie*, *Sir Patrick Spens*, *Edom of Gordon*, etc., etc. In these, if anywhere, we ought to find the traits that we seek to discover, for they, more than any other form of verse or prose, have not only been loved of the people, but, so far as we can see, must have come from the people itself. The "communal" theory of the ballad is a view that has little probability, but it is clear that the popular song and ballad had to a great extent a popular origin. I have already mentioned how this section of the *Oxford Book of English Verse* stands out from those that precede and follow it; it belongs altogether to a different school, with another outlook both on the world and on the art of poetry. If one could analyse fully the typical Scottish ballad on the one hand, and the typical English ballad on the other, it might not be so difficult to detect with certainty the northern note in English literature.

So much for the older poetry of the North. What of the prose? As regards that, it may safely be said that no prose-work in the older forms of northern English or Scottish deserves to be studied on account of any literary merit. It may be doubted whether any of the writers ever thought of such a thing as style, with the exception of Richard Rolle, who obviously gave considerable attention to rhythm and even to rhyme in his measured sentences. The only works which need to be considered in this connection are some of those produced in Scotland in the sixteenth and seventeenth centuries dealing with events of contemporary history, such as John Knox's *History of the Reformation*, and its continuation, the *Memorials* of his secretary, Richard Bannatyne, the *Chronicles* of Lindsay of Pitscottie, the *Diurnal of Occurrents*, or the history of the *Troubles in Scotland*, by George Spalding. The authors of

these and similar works obviously gave little heed
to the form of their narrative, but they often have
a rugged forcefulness, a plain bluntness, a feeling
for the picturesque and the dramatic, that makes
amends for the defects and intricacies of their
style. They are especially successful in the
delineation of character, for their interest is often
personal rather than broadly historical, and from
their works an interesting study could be made of
Scottish types for comparison with those of the
later Scottish novelists. They also present a
striking picture of Scottish culture (or the lack of
it) at that period. Almost any twenty pages of
Spalding's *Troubles* will show how late the northern
parts of Scotland were in attaining to a state of
law and order, and will explain how easily certain
primitive traits could survive long enough to place
their stamp on the literature of a later day.

Towards the end of the seventeenth century a
new period in northern literature begins. The
various dialects, which had been assuming their
modern forms during the two or three previous
centuries, begin to be used in writing, with a
deliberate effort to produce something more
natural, something with a more direct and intimate
appeal to the reader or hearer, than any composition in standard English could do. It is significant
that this movement begins in the North. Yorkshire and Scotland anticipated the South by some-

thing like a half a century. The North of England began poorly, and in spite of occasional local successes, has not yet succeeded in producing a dialect-literature of sufficient merit to compel attention or admiration from the outside world. It is worth noting, however, that in a bibliography of English dialect-works the share of the six northern counties is three-fourths of the whole, and that two of these, Lancashire and Yorkshire, have produced more than all the rest of England. It is not quantity that is lacking, but quality. Scotland had not only a better start, with Robert and Francis Semple, the two Hamiltons, and Allan Ramsay, but was able to rise to greater heights in a long line of poets and prose-writers, unbroken to the present day. Here, also, there is copious material for study, though not all of it can be taken as evidence. Allan Ramsay, for instance, was only in part original in his choice and treatment of themes; to a considerable extent he was under the influence of the classicism that prevailed in English poetry of the time. His *Gentle Shepherd* is a Scottish pastoral largely because the scene is laid in Scotland and the language is Scottish. With a change of the scene and the dialect, no radical re-casting would be necessary to convert it into an English pastoral staged in Kent or Devon.

It is unnecessary to trace the further progress of Scottish dialect-poetry from Ramsay to its culmination in Burns, as the advance is not so much in kind as in quality. The one new feature of importance which appears before the close of the eighteenth century is the Jacobite song, for attachment to the Stuarts involved some admiration for the Highlanders who were their last hope, and helped to change the sentiments of the Lowlanders towards their traditional enemies—a change which was naturally assisted by the fact that the old reasons for dislike had also largely disappeared with the breaking up of the clan-system and the opening up of the Highlands.

Lecture II

IF this extensive northern literature is critically examined, and an attempt made to discover its distinguishing features, there are certain points which at once force themselves on the attention, and a brief survey of these will enable us to see which of them have been carried over into the newer literature which is mainly written in standard English, or have influenced the matter and form of these later works.

In spite of the sarcastic remarks of the author of the *Owl and Nightingale*, charging the North with a lack of musical knowledge, northern poetry has from the beginning been distinguished by a keen sense of form, a remarkable skill in the handling of metre, and a strong tendency to the use of elaborate rhyming and alliterative devices. These qualities appear distinctly in some of the earliest pieces, in the romance of *Sir Tristrem*, for example, which Robert of Brunne (who had no doubt that it was composed by Thomas of Erceldoun) considered the best of all romances, but complained that the stanza was too elaborate for the ordinary minstrel to remember. It is probably not an accident that of all the poems in the English tongue the one which exhibits the highest degree of elaboration in metrical structure, the *Pearl*, belongs to the northern area and contains a remarkable number of Scandinavian words. It is true that these features are not entirely confined to the North, but their prevalence there is noteworthy, especially when we remember that the northern poets never lost the tradition of exact metre, which broke down in the South in the early years of the fifteenth century and was not recovered until towards the middle of the sixteenth. The recovery may have been largely due to foreign influences, but it is also possible that, in the case of Surrey, the close study of Douglas's Virgil was not without its effect. In addition to this exactness of form, the Scottish poets of the later fifteenth and the sixteenth centuries show a fondness for complicated rhyming, on internal as well as terminal syllables, which is very rare in English, although examples may be found in the earlier period. This can easily be carried to excess, and result in the production of mere rhyme instead of poetry, but the desire to do it at all shows to what extent the idea of form held its ground in the North.

Another feature of the best northern poetry is a fondness for rapid movement, which frequently, though not necessarily, leads to a remarkable conciseness and definiteness in the presentation. There is, without question, abundance of leisurely versification in the North as well as in the South, but mainly in the metrical homilies, lives of saints, and similar works, or in the productions of ecclesiastical writers like Barbour and Wyntoun, accustomed to bestow all their tediousness upon their hearers. The romances are, however, of another kind. Their authors have a story to tell, and they have no intention of allowing the hearer's interest to flag. The *Tristrem* is again an example of this, combining its elaborate stanza with a brevity of statement which often renders the narrative obscure. In this instance the rapid movement is achieved by the use of a very short line, but the effect was also attained by means of the long alliterative line, which rushes on with the rapid flow of a mountain stream, and in which only a dull poet can produce really dull verse. It is significant that much of the Middle English alliterative poetry is northern, and particularly that the North can lay claim to all that set of poems in which the alliterative lines are combined in stanza form, tailing off in the last four or five lines to an effective close. This type was in favour on both sides of the Border, but survived longest in Scotland, where it came at last to an ignominious, but still vigorous, end in the *Flyting* between Polwart and Montgomery. As an example of what it can be at its best, no finer passage can be found than that in the *Buke of the Howlat* which describes the arms of the Douglas and the story of Bruce's heart—a passage of 170 lines for which it would be in vain to seek a parallel in southern English poetry before the later years of the sixteenth century.

The sudden outburst of alliterative verse in the fourteenth century presents a problem for which various solutions have been suggested. As likely as any of these is the possibility that the northern poet saw in it a means of expressing himself with greater vigour and swiftness than could be attained by the ordinary rhyming line of alternate beats. What supplied him with the idea, and provided him with models is not quite clear, though the place held by Scandinavian words in some of the poems may be significant.

A different method of achieving this rapidity of movement presents itself in Blind Harry's *Wallace*. Here the medium is not the metre itself, which is the ordinary rhyming couplet of ten syllables, but the determination of the poet not to be diffuse or to be tempted into any long digression from his main theme. He always becomes impatient when he has to speak of any incident not closely connected with this, and dismisses it with such phrases as, "What suld I speik of frustir", "On to my tale I left", "To my matter now will I briefly wend". To be "prolix" was clearly a fault which he was determined to avoid. Hence he excels in concise and vivid narrative, as in the account of the pursuit of Wallace in the fifth book, where the lines become quick and breathless like the chase itself, and yet admit of such definite touches as the mention of Wallace leaving his exhausted horse "beside the standand stanes".

This love of conciseness, the avoidance of all unnecessary explanation or comment, the selection of a salient feature, and the expressing of it in a brief and telling phrase, are above all evident in the ballads, where they are an essential part of the technique. Whatever may have been the ultimate source of the ballad or the ballad style, this feature of it was one which suited the temperament of the northern poets, who had no difficulty in acquiring the art of its successful use. Many ballads, taken as a whole, have obvious weaknesses, but there are few which do not contain verses or lines of super-lative merit because of this one quality. Take, for example, in the ballad of *Johnny Armstrong*, the verse with which the borderer finally replies to the king's rejection of all his offers to ransom himself:

> To seek het water beneath cauld ice,
> Surely it is a great folie;
> I have asked grace at a graceless face,
> But there is nane for my men and me.

To show the point to which this conciseness can be carried, there is no better example than the brief ballad which relates to the burning of the castle of Auchindoun. Here, in no more than four stanzas, we have first the attempt of some un-named person to dissuade the resolute Highlander from the act, and his determined refusal to be turned from his purpose. Then, with exact localization, the testimony of an eyewitness of the scene presented by the blazing castle. This is how the author conveys the tale in the space of sixteen short lines:

> "Turn, Willie Mackintosh,
> Turn, turn, I bid you,
> Gin ye burn Auchindoun,
> Huntly will head you."

> "Head me or hang me,
> That winna fley me,
> I'll burn Auchindoun,
> Ere the life lea' me."

> Comin' ower Cairn Croom,
> An' lookin' doun, man,
> I saw Willie Mackintosh
> Burn Auchindoun, man.

> Comin' doun Deeside
> In a clear dawin',
> Auchindoun was in flames
> Ere the cock-crawin'.

It is not only in the ballad that we find this art displayed. It can appear in briefer pieces of verse,

which have all the conciseness of an epigram,
although they belong to a totally different type of
poetry. Some of them are artless enough, the
compositions of men and women unaccustomed to
express themselves in verse, but spurred on to do
so by some special incident or emotion. Such are
the few lines in which the tragedy of three lives
is summed up in these simple words:

> I never lo'ed a lad but twa,
>   Nor winna till I dee.
> The tane was killed in Lowren Fair,
>   The tither droun'd in Dee.
> An' they'll gang nae mare far Gadie rins
>   By the back o' Benachee.

That this simplicity, this directness, the avoidance of unnecessary detail, has something special
in it is shown by the failure of one great English
poet to appreciate it sufficiently. The tragic fate
of *Fair Helen of Kirkconnell* is beautifully told in
the well-known verses beginning "I wish I were
where Helen lies", and having for their refrain the
melodious line "On fair Kirkconnell Lee". The
details of the tragedy are rather suggested than
described, and with the exception of two stanzas
the poem is perfect of its kind. It is impossible to
understand how a poet like Wordsworth, while
recognizing that "it would be both presumptuous
and superfluous to attempt treating it in the same

4

way", should have conceived the idea of trans-
forming the story as he did in *Ellen Irwin*, introducing "at the outset a classical image to prepare
the reader for the style in which I meant to treat
the story, and so to preclude all comparison".
Comparison is, however, unavoidable, and has its
value in this connection, for there can be no more
instructive contrast between two totally different
conceptions of poetry than to set these two pieces
side by side, and compare, for example:

> Curst be the heart that thought the thought,
> And curst the hand that fired the shot,
> When in my arms burd Helen dropt,
>   And died to succour me,

with Wordsworth's corresponding lines:

> Proud Gordon cannot bear the thoughts
> That through his brain are travelling,—
> And starting up, to Bruce's heart
> He launched a deadly javelin.
> Fair Ellen saw it when it came,
> And stepping forth to meet the same,
> Did with her body cover
> The youth, her chosen lover.
>
> And, falling into Bruce's arms,
> Thus died the beauteous Ellen,
> Thus, from the heart of her true-love,
> The mortal spear repelling.

Surely there must be an essential difference between northern and southern conceptions of poetry before such a travesty was possible. Another argument for this difference might, indeed, be drawn from the converse case of Burns daring to rewrite Sir Robert Aytoun's dainty verses "I do confess thou'rt smooth and fair", with equally disastrous results, but with equal conviction that he had "improved the simplicity of the sentiments by giving them a Scots dress". So true is it that poets are seldom to be trusted when they express opinions on their own work.

The two short pieces of Scottish verse already quoted illustrate another feature which is distinctive of northern poetry, *viz.*, the frequency with which names of places are introduced, the obvious pleasure the poet takes in naming them, and the beauty which many of them give to the lines in which they occur. Even *Sir Tristrem* begins with a name of note, which has no connection with the story itself: "I was at Erceldoun, With Thomas spake I there", and the *Anturs of Arthure* enumerates the lands given to Sir Gawaine in such lines as "Cumnock and Carrick, Cunningham and Kyle". The subjects of the *Bruce*, the *Wallace*, and Wyntoun's *Chronicle* naturally call for the mention of many place-names, but these are inserted more frequently than English writers would have thought necessary, and frequently come in with good effect. It is instructive to note how frequently Dunbar uses the device in such pieces as his *Lament for the Makers*; even Lydgate is "the Monk of Bury", Henryson is linked with Dunfermline, while others are expressly designated by their locality—Clerk of Tranent, Roull of Aberdeen, Roull of Corstorphine, and the melodious "Sir Mungo Lockhart of the Lee".

It is in the ballads and songs, however, that the use of place-names comes in most copiously and most effectively. It is natural enough in the titles of many of the ballads, relating as they do to events or persons connected with certain localities, as in those already mentioned, but such instances are only a small number among the many that have no such imperative reason for their introduction. A glance over any collection of Scottish songs will show the surprising extent to which they are associated with definite localities. In Herd's collection of 1776, for instance, we find the following: The *Braes of Yarrow*, the *Broom of Cowden-knows*, the *Banks of Forth*, the *Bush aboon Traquair*, the *Birks of Invermay*, the *Braes of Ballenden*, the *Bonny Lass of Branksome*, the *Flowers of Edin-burgh*, *Polwart on the Green*, *Allan Water*, *Ettrick Banks*, *Leader Haughs*, *Roslin Castle*, *Tweed-side*, and so on.

At times, too, the poet is led by his theme to fill his verse with a series of place-names, and this, when skilfully done, brings out to the full the remarkable poetic effect which the mere names, in virtue both of their sound and their associations, can produce. This is something entirely different from the catalogue of river-names in the fourth book of Spenser's *Faery Queen*, or the methodical enumeration of names of places which runs all through Drayton's *Polyolbion*. One of the finest examples is the verse of *Leader Haughs*, in which the minstrel exclaims:

> Sing *Erceldoune* and *Cowdenknowes*,
>   Where Homes had ance commanding;
> And *Drygrange* with thy milk-white ewes,
>   Twixt *Tweed* and *Leader* standing.
> The birds that flees through *Reedpath* trees
>   And *Gledwood* banks ilk morrow,
> May chant and sing, sweet *Leader Haughs*,
>   And bonny howms of *Yarrow*.

In view of these models, it is obvious from what source Scott obtained the suggestion for the liberal use of place-names in his poems. Take, for instance, the night-ride of William of Deloraine in the *Lay of the Last Minstrel*, where his course is traced from Teviot-side, by the Peel of Goldiland, Borthwick, Hawick, Hazeldean, Horsliehill and the Roman Way, Minto Crags, and half a dozen more before he reaches Melrose. Compare this with the similar rapid course in the *Lady of the Lake*:

> Torry and Lendrick now are passed,
> And Deanstown lies behind them cast;
> They rise, the bannered towers of Doune, . . .
> Blair-Drummond sees the hoofs strike fire,
> They sweep like breeze through Ochtertyre; . . .

or in the *Bridal of Triermain*:

> Soon he crossed green Irthing's mead,
> Dashed o'er Kirkoswald's verdant plain,
> And Eden barred his course in vain,
> He passed red Penrith's Table Round, . . .
> Left Mayburgh's mound and stones of power. . . .
> And traced the Eamont's winding way,
> Till Ulfo's lake beneath him lay.

In such passages, it may be said, there is good reason for all the names, but in others the sheer delight of enumeration is obvious, as in *Marmion* where Sir David Lyndsay speaks of the phantom

> Seen in Rothiemurchus glade,
> Or where the sable pine-trees shade
> Dark Tomantoul, and Achnaslaid,
> Dromouchty, or Glenmore.

or again in the *Bridal of Triermain*

> Bewcastle now must keep the hold,
> Speir-Adam's steeds must bide in stall,
> Of Hartley-burn the bowmen bold
> Must only shoot from battled wall,
> And Liddesdale may buckle spur,
> And Teviot now may belt the brand,
> Tarras and Ewes keep nightly stir,
> And Eskdale foray Cumberland.

How thoroughly Scott carries out the tradition in
this respect is shown by the fact that in the first
four cantos of the *Lay of the Last Minstrel*, no less
than eighty names of places on both sides of the
Border occur.

Another Scottish poet who makes free use of
place-names is James Hogg, not only in his longer
poems, but in many of his shorter pieces and songs,
frequently introducing places of which he had no
personal knowledge, *e.g.*:

> The Tilt has vanished on the upland gray,
> The Tarf is dwindled to a foaming rill;
> The herd has crossed Breriach's gill,
> The Athol forest's formidable bound,
> And in the Garcharye a last retreat has found.

> Cauld is the blast on the braes of Strahonan,
> The top of Ben-Wevis is driftin' wi' snaw.

> Cam ye by Athol, lad wi' the philabeg,
> Down by the Tummel or banks o' the Garry?

> I sing of a land that was famous of yore,
> The land of green Appin, the ward of the flood.

> To the pine of Lochaber due honour be given.

It is a curious example of the effect of romanticism in effacing old differences that Hogg in his
Jacobite and other songs identifies himself so com-
pletely with the Highlands—a thing that no

Borderer of an earlier time would have dreamed
of doing.

More than forty years ago Professor Veitch
wrote at length on the *Feeling for Nature in Scottish
Poetry*, with copious extracts from the poets of all
the centuries, and it would be superfluous to add
anything to those aspects of the subject which he
has so fully treated in his two volumes.   Confining
his attention, however, to the professional or conventional poets, Professor Veitch omits to notice
one feature of Scottish popular poetry in relation
to natural scenery.   The authors of that poetry are
not interested in nature in the abstract; they must
have it embodied and localized.   Their imagination
is not excited, they are not impelled to poetic
expression, by the birch, the broom, or the heather
in themselves; what they delight to see and to put
in verse is the Broom of the Cowdenknowes and
the Birks of Invermay, or to recall "comin' ower
Munrimmon Muir amang the bonnie blumin'
heather".   One of the earliest pieces of Scottish
nature-poetry, composed by the middle of the
sixteenth century, illustrates this by its opening
line "Quhen Tayis bank wes blumit bricht" and its
closing couplet "Quhair Tay ran down with
stremis stout Full straucht under Stobschaw".

How the mind of the untutored poet works
here seems to me clearly indicated by two lines
of which I know no more than that I heard them

in my youth.   They may be a fragment of a longer piece, or there may never have been any more of them.   Their author had stood in the ravine known as the Den of Airlie, and there had heard the cuckoo calling, its notes sounding all the more loudly between the high wooded banks.   He had also known the open vale of Strathmore, and there had seen the white swan on the waters of a little lake, the Loch of Baikie.   And these two impressions he has recorded in the simple lines that do not even rhyme correctly:

> Loud cries the gouk in the high den o' Airlie,
> And bonnie swims the swan on the how loch o' Baikie.

The unstudied but exact contrast between each element in the two impressions, the one of sound and the other of sight, is an example of the artless art of the ballad or the song, which is so difficult to imitate because it is so deceptive in its seeming simplicity.   And each impression is made definite by being localized instead of being left as a vague generality.   If it is the function of the poet "to give to airy nothings a local habitation and a name", the Scottish minstrels certainly did not misunderstand their art.

2

One feature in which northern literature anticipates southern, and for which it shows a greater fondness, is in the realm of the supernatural.   It

was in all probability Grendel and Grendel's
mother, together with the fiery dragon, which
saved the *Beowulf* from being lost, for the compiler
of that manuscript was evidently a lover of the
marvellous. There are no similar figures in
Middle English literature till we come to the
Anturs of Arthur already referred to, where the
ghost of Queen Guenevere's mother appears,
ushered in by a real northern storm of rain and
snow among the rocky fells, and by a darkness
like that of an eclipse. This is, indeed, a "grisly
gaist", naked and bare, "beclaggèd in clay", with
eyes "glowing like gledes", and all the proper
accompaniments of toads and serpents that a sinful
soul from the other world ought to have, at the
sight of which even the greyhounds are aghast,
and the wild birds scream with fright. Another
early ghost is that of Fawdoun in Blind Harry's
Wallace, one of the hero's own followers, but
killed by him on suspicion of treachery. That
night Wallace and his men took up their quarters
in a deserted castle. As they sat there, they heard
horns blowing loudly outside, and one man after
another went to learn the cause, until Wallace
alone was left. When he in turn went to the
door, he found Fawdoun standing there with his
own head in his hands.

> In at Wallace the hede he swakkit thair;
> And he in haist sone hynt it by the hair,
> Syne out agayne at him he couth it cast.

Not until the Elizabethan dramatists bring their ghosts on the stage, do spectres of this kind play any part in English literature. Shakespeare, of course, does not confine his ghosts to the plays that are of northern origin, but it is significant that the two most impressive appear in *Macbeth* and *Hamlet*. In *Macbeth*, too, he not only took over the three hags from the Scottish legend, but by adopting their name as well—the weird sisters— was the means of bringing back into English a word which it had lost some two centuries before his time.

It is unnecessary, and would take too long, to discuss the supernatural in the ballads, with their ghosts like the two sons of the *Wife of Usher's Well*, or their glimpses of fairyland as in *Thomas the Rhymer*. Thomas himself is a figure which continued for five or six centuries to dominate Scottish tradition; and akin to his gift of prophecy, for which he is cited by early writers like Barbour, Wyntoun, and Blind Harry, is that other gift of *second sight*, which owes its name as well as its notoriety to Scotland. Made known to English readers by such writers as Captain Burt (who boldly denounced it as a "cheat" and the second-sighted persons as "imposters") and Pennant, it was inevitable that Scott should introduce it in the *Lady of the Lake* and *Waverley*. In the former, no doubt is cast on old Allan Bane's honesty, but in *Waverley* the effect of Captain Burt's scepticism is evident. "Is not his son Malcolm a *taishatr* (a second-sighted person)?" asked Evan. "Nothing equal to his father", replied Donald Bean. "He told us the other day we were to see a great gentleman riding on a horse, and there came nobody that whole day but Shemis Beg, the blind harper with his dog." In the *Legend of Montrose*, it will be remembered, part of the plot turns upon the possession of this gift by Allan MacAulay. Thomas Campbell, too, made good use of it in *Lochiel's Warning*, which is a dialogue between the seer and his chief:

> For a field of the dead rushes red on my sight,
> And the clans of Culloden are scattered in flight. . .
>
> 'Tis the sunset of life gives me mystical lore,
> And coming events cast their shadows before.

It was natural that Scott, with his intense interest in such themes and his knowledge of the literature relating to them, should introduce them freely into his own works. An extensive study of popular beliefs could be made from his poems and the Waverley novels, and for some of them a long pedigree could be made out. The stanza in the fifth canto of *Marmion* beginning with the lines

> Dun-Edin's cross, a pillared stone,
> Rose on a turret octagon,

and giving an account of the mysterious summons containing the roll of names of those who were to perish at Flodden, was derived from the *Chronicles* of Pitscottie, who tells the tale with some common-sense doubts, but without questioning the reality of the incident.

> In this mean time there was a cry heard at the Market Cross of Edinburgh at the hour of midnight, proclaiming as it had been a summons, which was called by the proclaimer thereof the summons of Plotcok, which desired all men to compear, both earl, lord, baron, and gentleman, and all honest burgesses within the town, every man specified by his own name to compear within the space of fourty days before his master, where it shall happen him to appoint.
>
> Whether this summons was proclaimed by vain persons, night walkers or drunken men for their pastime, or if it was a spirit I cannot tell truly; but it was shown to me that a noble man of the town called Master Richard Lawson, being evil disposed, going in his gallery stair fornent the cross, hearing the voice proclaiming this summons, thought marvel what it should be, and cried on his servant to bring him his purse. When he had brought it, he took out a crown, and cast it over the stair, saying those words: "I appeal from that summons, judgement and sentence thereof, and betake me all whole in the mercy of God and Christ Jesus, his Son."

Pitscottie's informant, who was in Edinburgh at the time of the incident, assured him that at the Field of Flodden "there was no manner of man that was called in that summons that escaped, but that man alone who maid his protestation and appealed". All the rest perished in the battle along with their king.

The fact that a similar story is told in one of the chapters of *Njáls Saga* might well suggest that it is of northern origin, but this is disproved by its occurrence centuries before in the *Dialogues* of Gregory the Great. The Scottish version is original, however, in the formal protest made by the ready-minded burgess, and his consequent escape from the fate of all the rest. It is an example of the practical Scottish character asserting itself even in the face of the supernatural, as it does in the ballad of *Thomas the Rhymer* when the Queen of Elfland confers on him the gift of "the tongue that can never lee".

> "My tongue is my ain", true Thomas said,
>   "A gudely gift ye wad gie to me!
> I neither dought to buy or sell,
>   At fair or tryst where I may be."

3

It is, no doubt, accidental that the record of Scottish poetry begins with a lament, in the eight lines on the state of Scotland after the death of Alexander the Third. The older poets, however, are liberal in laments and complaints, some purely conventional, others full of real feeling, and in the later and more popular poetry there are few finer pieces than those which spring from some deep sorrow or regret for things past. The *Dowie Dens of Yarrow*, the *Flowers of the Forest*, *Lochaber No More*, *Fair Helen of Kirkconnell* are of one type; *Lady Anne Bothwell's Lament*, *O, Walie, Walie, Ye Banks and Braes o' Bonnie Doon* are of another. Even the piece which boasts the beauties of Leader Haughs and Yarrow ends with a note of sorrow.

> But minstrel Burn cannot assuage
>   His grief, while life endureth,
> To see the changes of this age,
>   That fleeting time procureth;
> For mony a place stands in hard case,
>   Where blythe fowk kend nae sorrow,
> With Homes that dwelt on Leader side,
>   And Scotts that dwelt on Yarrow.

If there is any justification for tracing Celtic influence in Lowland Scottish poetry, it may be here that it is to be found, for Gaelic poetry is also rich in similar themes from the seventeenth century down to the present day. The *cumha* or lament, and the *marbhrann* or elegy, are among the most usual types of Gaelic verse, and some are inimitable for the harmony of the sound with the feeling that the words convey. Such a piece as William Ross's *Cuachag nan craobh* is a masterpiece of this kind.

It was with some reason that James Macpherson,
taking his cue from the well-known tradition of
Oisean an deigh na Feinne, and familiar with
contemporary Gaelic poetry, shrouded the heroes
and heroines of his Ossianic poems in a veil of
mist and melancholy. It was one-sided and over-
done, but there was something to justify it.

Of any direct influence of that Gaelic poetry
upon Lowland Scottish, there is no evidence, and
little likelihood. The two literatures existed side
by side without actual contact; the barrier of
language was too great for the Lowlander to
penetrate. For at least a century, from 1640
onwards, Highland poets and poetesses were producing finer and more original verse than anyone
in the Lowlands. The war-songs and satirical
verses of Iain Lóm, the elegies of Mary Macleod,
the varied productions of Alexander MacDonald,
the nature poetry of Duncan Ban Macintyre, have
no parallels in the contemporary dialect-poetry of
Scotland. This availed nothing when no Lowlander could read them, and when a Highlander
like Macpherson chose rather to exploit his own
fancies than to do justice to the real literature of
his people. It was not until the second half of the
nineteenth century that readers ignorant of Gaelic
had much opportunity of gaining, through translations, some idea of the nature of this modern
Gaelic poetry. When Scott, in *Waverley* and the

Legend of Montrose, professed to give English renderings of Gaelic songs, he made no effort whatever to produce something which might pass for a real translation from that language, and plainly indicated this by the remarks with which the so-called "translations" were accompanied.

Lecture III

IT was suggested in the first lecture that to look
for northern traits in English literature prior
to the eighteenth century might almost be set
down as a forlorn quest. This, however, is by no
means to be assumed without further inquiry.
The classical Latin writers worked largely upon
Greek models, and even on Greek subjects, but
they produced a literature which is essentially
Roman in character and not Greek. It is equally
possible that the Anglo-Saxons and their descen-
dants, while writing under southern influences and
on southern themes, may have been successful in
imbuing their literature with their own spirit and
making it a true expression of their own character.
The Anglo-Saxons were a northern race, and it
may be contended that whatever can be called
truly English in the earlier or later literature can
legitimately be claimed as a manifestation of the
northern spirit.

This may be true in the abstract, but in carrying theory into practice, and endeavouring to
identify what is truly English or northern, it is
necessary to proceed with caution. Above all, it
is imperative to start without prejudice, without

any preconceived ideas as to what is natural or
peculiar to the North in contrast to the South.
Otherwise we shall fall into the fallacy of those who
believe that certain features in English literature
are typically Celtic, and then claim for the Celt
every piece of English verse or prose which presents
these characteristics—a fallacy which is represented
in its extreme form in such collections as William
Sharp's *Lyra Celtica*. It might equally well be
argued that, if the feature in question is widely
represented in English, the probability is that it is
not exclusively Celtic in origin, however prominent
it may be in that literature.

Any inquiry of this nature may naturally begin
with Anglo-Saxon poetry, and with the question
whether any special features of this can be assumed
to be purely or prominently northern. Some
obvious characteristics, to which that poetry owes
much of its vigour and colour, might seem at first
to claim a place in this respect, but further consideration makes it difficult to allow that they can
be properly entitled to it. Anglo-Saxon poetry,
not only on Germanic themes, but even on those
of Scriptural and early Christian origin, is marked
by a fondness for depicting scenes of warfare and
sea-faring, which clearly indicates that each of
these manly activities appealed strongly to the poet
and his audience. It is obvious that we have here
a genuinely original Germanic interest, which sets

an unmistakeable stamp upon much of the Anglo-
Saxon poet's work, appearing no less in the *Genesis*
and *Exodus*, the *Andreas* and *Elene*, than in the
battles of Brunanburh and Maldon, the *Wanderer*
and *Seafarer*. Warfare and voyaging, however,
were neither the invention of the Germanic peoples,
nor an interest peculiar to their poets; they were
occupations equally familiar to the Greeks and the
Romans, and no less favourite subjects with the
authors of the *Iliad* and *Odyssey*, of the *Aeneid*
and *Pharsalia*. Unless it can be demonstrated
that the Anglo-Saxon poet had a different outlook
on battles and the sea, and had developed a
different method of interpreting his conception of
them, it is difficult to maintain that in this respect
his work is characteristically northern. All that we
can say is that in recognizing these two themes as
being of the highest interest to his audience, he is
addressing himself to men of northern race, to
whom, as to other races, they were matters of
ordinary and daily experience.

One other feature of Anglo-Saxon poetry has
more claim to consideration here. The devotion
of follower to leader, of the ordinary fighting-man
to his war-chief, is a trait of early Germanic society
which, if not lacking, is not prominent in Greek
and Latin poetry. We find it not only in the
Beowulf where Wiglaf shows his devotion to his
lord and heaps reproaches on those who fail him

in his hour of need, or in the *Battle of Maldon*, where one man after another falls, disdaining to survive the leader whom he had sworn to stand by to the last, but we have it nobly stated in the *Andreas*, when Andrew suggests that his companions should leave him to go on the perilous voyage alone. They answer:

> Whither can we go without our lord, mournful of mood and of good devoid. . .If we fail thee, we shall be odious in every land, despised by the people, when the brave sons of men sit and debate as to which of them ever stood best by his lord in the fight, when hand and shield suffered straits on the battle-field, ground down by bills in the hostile play.

The same feeling finds similar expression in the Old Saxon *Hêliand*,where the disciple Thomas uses similar language when Jesus declares his intention of returning among the Jews.

> Let us stay with him and suffer with our prince. That is the merit of a thane that he stand fast by his lord and die with him there in honour. Let us all do so, and follow him in this journey. Let us not reckon our lives of any worth, unless we die in the host along with him, our lord. Then our glory will live after us, our good name among men.

The replacing of the old Germanic type of society by the feudal system did not alter this attachment of the follower to his chief. As late as the sixteenth century the idea is still clearly expressed in Scottish poetry, when a father, among

other sage counsels given to his son, instructs him
in lines which may be partly englished thus:

> Flee thou never thy master fro,
> For thou shalt suffer meikle wo.
> And since thou knowest thou must die,
> What boot is there from death to fly?
> Where may'st thou die with more honoúr,
> Than with thy master in a stour?..
> For if thou flee from him to town,
> I give thee, son, my malison.
> Rather on thee thy death thou take,
> Than flee and thy good lord forsake.[1]

In later literature this devotion is characteristic
of the Highlands of Scotland, in the relationship
between clansman and chief. This was natural
from the very nature of the clan system, originating as it did in the gathering of a number of fighting
men round a man of mark as their leader, frequently, as the names indicate, one of Scandinavian
descent.   "The ordinary Highlanders", wrote
Captain Burt, "esteem it the most sublime degree
of virtue to love their chief, and pay him a blind
obedience, although it be in opposition to the
Government, the laws of the kingdom, or even to
the law of God."[2]   As an instance of this attachment and fidelity, he tells the story of one who
at the Battle of Glenshiels in 1719, sheltered his

[1] *The Maitland Folio Manuscript* (Scottish Text Society, 1919), vol.
I, p. 172.
[2] Burt, *Letters from the North* (ed. 1876), vol. II, letter xix, pp. 117-8.

fallen chief with his own body, receiving several wounds from bullets aimed at his master. Whatever faults the Highlander may have had, and in the eyes of the Lowlander he had many, this was one quality which could not be denied to him. In the epitaph of one who was a kind of Rob Roy in Sutherland in the eighteenth century, it comes in triumphantly as the great virtue which could be set against anything unfavourable to his memory:

> Donald MacMurrochy here lies low,
> Was ill to his freind and war to his foe,
> But true to his master in weill and woe.

It was inevitable, when the romantic view of Highland character became the prevailing one, that this devotion to the chief should be selected as one of the finest traits. Scott, it will be remembered, makes use of it at the trial of Fergus MacIvor, when Evan MacCombich offers himself and any six of the best of the clan as a substitute for his chief, and silences the amusement in court with the words: "If they laugh because they think I would not keep my word, and come back to redeem him, I can tell them they ken neither the heart of a Hielandman, nor the honour of a gentleman."[1]

Beyond the general disparagement of the Scots which has already been mentioned, there is little

[1]Scott, *Waverley*, chap. lxviii.

in the older literature of England to indicate any views on the character of the northern man. The two Yorkshire youths who figure in the *Reeve's Tale* of Chaucer have nothing distinctive about them, except their speech, which gives a certain touch of local colour. In Bullein's *Dialogue* already mentioned, the common estimate of the Borderer, whether English or Scottish, is conveyed by the beggar's description of himself as having been "born in Redesdale in Northumberland, and come of a wight riding sirname called the Robsons, good honest men and true, saving a little shifting for their living". The beadle of the beggars, he explains, was also "a Redesdale man born, a good man and true, which for ill will in his youth did fleem the countrie; it was laid to his charge the driving of kine hame to his father's byre."

The general lack of northern themes, however, in English literature of the fifteenth and sixteenth centuries made it unnecessary for writers to express, either in prose or verse, any ideas they may have had on the subject of northern character. In this respect the older Scottish literature is more interesting and enlightening. The long poems of Barbour and Blind Harry, in addition to the history they relate, provide striking character-studies of Bruce, Douglas, Wallace, and other famous Scots, either drawn at large, as in the case of the principal actors, or brought out by some

incident in which they take part. Such detailed
portraits as those of Bruce or Wallace are no
conventional descriptions; they are consistent
presentations of real persons, differing in many
respects from each other, and deliberately contrasted by Blind Harry in more than one passage.
Wyntoun's unknown contributor, with no opportunity for this detailed portraiture, has several
anecdotes which illustrate various traits of Scottish
character. One is of Sir Andrew Murray, who
with a small company of followers was hearing
mass, when an English force was seen approaching.
No one ventured to tell Sir Andrew until the mass
was over, and then his reply was: "No haste."
As he was about to mount his horse, one of the
leather thongs of his armour broke. He coolly
called for a small box, took out of it a piece of
skin, from which he deliberately cut a new thong,
and only after he had mended the defect did he
begin to lead off his men. "I have heard several
worthy knights", adds the writer, "say that never
in all their days did they have so uncomfortable
waiting as in the cutting of that thong."[1] This is
really an admirable picture of the imperturbable
Scot, declining to be hurried on any account.

The same Sir Andrew was marching north to
relieve the castle of Kildrummie in Aberdeenshire,
which was besieged by David, Earl of Athole.

[1] *The Orygynale Cronikil*, bk. viii, ll. 4782-4810.

The two forces met in a narrow way where there was a great stone, to which Earl David addressed the words: "By God's face, we two shall take to flight together."[1]   Scott, who had read Wyntoun attentively, no doubt had this in mind when he wrote:

> Come one, come all, this rock shall fly
> From its firm base as soon as I.

He was certainly following the account of the wounded Highlander at the Battle of Gasclune in 1392, when he attributed the death of Sir Giles de Argentine at Bannockburn to the fierce stroke of the "grim lord of Colinsay".[2]

It might be argued that no special importance attaches to the fact that older Scottish literature presents a larger number of these studies of character than the English of the same period— that this is an accident arising from the lack of southern works of the same type.   This very fact, however, seems to me significant.   There is abundance of historical matter in English during these centuries, but it is of a different nature—more historical, perhaps, but less personal.   The Scottish writers here have interests akin to those of the Icelandic saga-tellers; they are interested in the life-story of their heroes, when they deal with these at length, and in separate incidents which have a

[1]*Ibid.*, ll. 4669-4772.
[2]Scott, *Lord of the Isles*, canto vi, stanza 32.

real point, out of which a story can be made. The ability to catch an unusual or humorous situation, and to relate it in an effective way, is still notably common among all classes in Scotland, and is the source of the inexhaustible fund of Scottish anecdote. In this, it seems to me, we have a distinct northern characteristic, accounting for a striking difference between the two literatures in the older period.

To return for a little to the appreciation of the northern character, it might have been expected that the intensive cultivation of the drama in the seventeenth century, and the beginnings of the novel, would before long have led to the introduction of northern characters in both of these species of writing. Their absence shows that even the Union of the Crowns had failed to turn literature in this direction; not even the motive of gaining royal favour was strong enough to break through the traditional disregard of this theme. The result is that the first author, to all appearance, who has a good word to say of Scotland, was himself a Scot— the precocious and far-travelled William Lithgow. His panegyric is ample enough to make up for the previous conspiracy of silence. In her *Welcome to her Native Son, King Charles* written in 1633, Scotland thus sings her own praises:

> Look to my valour past, and thou may'st spy
> Where diverse nations got of me supply.

France can approve my manhood. I relieved
Their state from thralldom when it was surgrieved.
Witness our mutual league; witness their guard,
And mine there naturalized for my reward.

Like, Belgians swear their strength, their stoutest hand,
And warriors best, are bred within my land.
The Almaynes too record what I have done,
And what my soldiers anciently there won.
Look to my sister Swethland, and behold
What birth I send them, desperate, stout, and bold.
For Poland, she's my nurse, brings up my youth,
Full thirty thousand yearly, of a truth;
Then loads them with the fatness of her soil,
Which I, in their due time, do still recoil.
Then look to Denmark, where twelve thousands lie,
Serving thine uncle, sharpest fortunes try.

Last step I o'er to Ireland, and do see
Full forty thousand Scots, armed men, there be.
Besides at home one hundred thousands mo,
Young, stout, and strong, well-armed for thee, to go
To challenge destiny, and cruel fate,
And all usurpers, dare menace my state.

In these lines Lithgow anticipated by almost
a century the eulogy of another Scot, James
Thomson, whose praise of his country was all the
more important because so much more widely
known. Lithgow's verse was probably read by
very few; Thomson's *Seasons* were read and
admired by many, and these numerous readers

found in his *Autumn* these lines in praise of Scotland:

>   And here a while the Muse,
> High-hovering o'er the broad cerulean scene,
> Sees Caledonia in romantic view:
> Her airy mountains, from the waving main
> Invested with a keen diffusive sky,
> Breathing the soul acute; her forests huge,
> Incult, robust, and tall, by nature's hand
> Planted of old; her azure lakes between
> Poured out extensive, and of watery wealth
> Full; winding deep and green, her fertile vales,
> With many a cool translucent brimming flood
> Washed lovely, from the Tweed (pure parent-stream,
> Whose pastoral banks first heard my Doric reed,
> With, silvan Jed, thy tributary brook),
> To where the north-inflated tempest foams
> O'er Orca's or Betubium's highest peak.
> Nurse of a people, in misfortune's school
> Trained up to hardy deeds; soon visited
> By Learning, when before the Gothic rage
> She took her western flight. A manly race,
> Of unsubmitting spirit, wise and brave,
> Who still through bleeding ages struggled hard
> (As well unhappy Wallace can attest,
> Great patriot hero, ill-requited chief)
> To hold a generous undiminished state;
> Too much in vain! Hence of unequal bounds
> Impatient, and by tempting glory borne
> O'er every land, for every land their life
> Has flowed profuse, their piercing genius planned,
> And swelled the pomp of peace their faithful toil,
> As from their own clear north, in radiant streams,
> Bright over Europe bursts the Boreal Morn.

2

Considering the nature of the mountainous parts of England and Scotland before the eighteenth century, the lack of roads, the absence of cultivation, and the reputation of the inhabitants, it is not surprising that no enthusiasm was felt for them by those who lived in the more level, fertile, and cultured areas. This is excellently brought out by Scott in the second chapter of the *Legend of Montrose*:

> It was towards the close of a summer's evening . . . that a young gentleman of quality, well mounted and armed, and accompanied by two servants , . . rode slowly up one of those steep passes by which the Highlands are accessible from the Lowlands of Perthshire. Their course had lain for some time along the banks of a lake, whose deep waters reflected the crimson beams of the western sun. The broken path which they pursued, with some difficulty, was in some places, shaded by ancient birches and oak trees, and in others overhung by fragments of huge rock. Elsewhere, the hill, which formed the northern side of this beautiful sheet of water, arose in steep but less precipitous acclivity, and was arrayed in heath of the darkest purple. In the present times a scene so romantic would have been judged to possess the highest charms for the traveller; but those who journey in days of doubt and dread pay little attention to picturesque scenery.

The lack of interest or appreciation for mountain scenery is plainly evident in such a work as

Drayton's *Polyolbion*. In the last four books of this, containing a description of the six northern counties, the poet succeeds in writing some sixteen hundred lines of verse with only brief and occasional mention of this theme, the most notable exceptions being the speech of Skiddaw in the thirtieth 'Song', and when the rugged ground in one place suggests to him that there might be mineral wealth beneath it.

> Than Copland, of this tract a corner, I would know
> What place can there be found in Britain that doth show
> A surface more austere, more stern from every way,
> That who doth it behold, he cannot choose but say,
> Th' aspect of these grim hills, these stark and misty dales,
> From clouds scarce ever clear'd with the strong'st northern gales,
> Tell in their mighty roots some mineral there doth lie,
> The island's general want whose plenty might supply.[1]

We have to wait long after this to find an English poet differently affected by mountain-scenery. In 1739 Gray expressed his admiration of the Alps, though still qualifying it with the conventional adjectives: "You here meet with all the beauties so savage and horrid a place can present you with." Thirty years later he was still more attracted by the grandeur of the Lake

[1]Drayton, *Polyolbion*, song 30.

Country. In contrast to this it is interesting to cite the opinions of Captain Burt, one of whose letters is mainly devoted to an account of the Highland hills, and contains such passages as these:

> I shall soon conclude this description of the outward appearance of the mountains, which I am already tired of as a disagreeable subject, and I believe you are so too; but for your future ease in that particular, there is not much variety in it but gloomy spaces, different rocks, and heath, and high and low.
>
> To cast one's eye from one eminence toward a group of them they appear still one above another , . . and the whole of a dismal gloomy brown drawing upon a dirty purple, and most of all disagreeable when the heath is in bloom.
>
> But of all the views, I think the most horrid is, to look at the hills from east to west, or *vice versâ*, for then the eye penetrates far among them, and sees more particularly their tremendous bulk, frightful irregularity, and horrid gloom.[1]

In conclusion, he contrasts these gloomy heights, very much to their disadvantage, with a real "poetical mountain"—Richmond Hill.

About the time that these remarks of Captain Burt appeared in print, the unlettered forester of Glenorchy, Duncan Ban Macintyre, was composing two of the finest pieces of modern Gaelic poetry, *Beinn Dorain* and *Coire Cheathaich*, minute descriptions of a hill and of a mountain hollow, in

[1]Burt, *Letters from the North*, vol. II, letter **xv**, pp. 32-36.

which, if anywhere, a true love of the beauty of the
hills breathes in every line.   What Duncan felt
and expressed by intimate contact with the wild
nature among which he had grown up, the cultured
world of the South was only beginning to appreciate.   There were few who were inspired by the
enthusiasm which Collins expresses in his *Ode*:

> All hail, ye scenes that o'er my soul prevail!
>   Ye splendid firths and lakes, which, far away,
>   Are by smooth Annan filled, or past'ral Tay,
> Or Don's romantic springs, at distance, hail!
> The time shall come, when I perhaps may tread
>   Your lowly glens o'erhung with spreading broom,
> Or o'er your stretching heaths, by Fancy led,
>   Or o'er your mountains creep, in awful gloom!
> Then will I dress once more the faded bower,
>   Where Jonson sat in Drummond's classic shade,
> Or crop from Tiviotdale each lyric flower,
>   And mourn, on Yarrow's banks, where Willy's laid.

Some of the appreciation of the wild scenery of
the Highlands came through the one-sided but
impressive idea of them conveyed by Macpherson's
Ossian.   This is correctly summed up by Dr. Hugh
Blair, in these words: "The scenery throughout
wild and romantic.   The extended heath by the
seashore; the mountains shaded with mist; the
torrent rushing through a solitary valley, the
scattered oaks, and the tombs of warriors over-
grown with moss."   That, of course, fitted in with

6

the taste of the day, which on the one hand would
have seen nothing romantic in mountains and
glens rich in verdure, or in the bloom of the heather
bathed in sunshine, and on the other was inclined
to admire nature in proportion as it approximated
to something regular and artificial.   This is
apparent even in the lines written by Burns at
Kenmore, Taymouth, in 1787, where, after describ-
ing the wilder scenery in these lines:

> Admiring Nature in her wildest grace,
> My savage journey curious I pursue. . . .
> The meeting cliffs a deep-sunk glen divides,
> The woods, wild-scattered, clothe their ample sides;
> The outstretching lake, embosom'd 'mong the hills,
> The eye with wonder and amazement fills;—

he dwells upon the milder aspects of the scene:

> The Tay, meandering sweet in infant pride,
> The palace rising on his verdant side,
> The lawns, wood-fringed in Nature's native taste,
> The hillocks, dropt in Nature's careless haste,
> The arches, striding o'er the new-born stream,
> The village, glittering in the noontide beam.

Although Gray began by admiring the Alps,
and Wordsworth's first descriptions of mountain
scenery were written in Switzerland, the part
played by the North in developing the appreciation
of this aspect of nature is unmistakable.   This
appears clearly in William Gilpin's *Observations*

Relative Chiefly to Picturesque Beauty, which are mainly the record of his tours in the Lake District and in the Scottish Highlands. It is true that Gilpin's appreciation was limited; he was prepared to admire a mountain only if it conformed to his ideas of form and colour, and was of opinion that it was only in the distance that "the mountain properly appears, where ... its monstrous features, losing their deformity, assume a softness which naturally belongs to them". He also thought that "the mountains of Sweden, Norway, and other Northern regions, are probably rather masses of hideous rudeness than scenes of grandeur and proportion". When these lines were written, artist and poet were largely in agreement, but within a few years the poet and the novelist had invested the northern hills with unqualified grandeur and beauty, and with them had introduced a new element into English literature.

The credit of this change is shared by both Scott and Wordsworth, in whose poetry the theme of the hills appears almost simultaneously. Scott in his *Lay of the Last Minstrel* had briefly touched the note in the familiar lines:

> O Caledonia, stern and wild. . .
> Land of brown heath and shaggy wood,
> Land of the mountain and the flood,
> Land of my sires, what mortal hand
> Can e'er untie the filial band,
> That knits me to thy rugged strand.

In the *Lady of the Lake* the whole setting of the tale required that the landscape should be invested with the hues of romance, and so it is from the very opening of the poem:

> The stag at eve had drunk his fill,
> Where danced the moon on Monan's rill,
> And deep his midnight lair had made
> In lone Glenartney's hazel shade.

The stanzas that follow upon the close of the chase, beginning with

> The western waves of ebbing day
> Rolled o'er the glen their level way,

present a combined picture of hill and wood, of rock and lake, more complete and more perfect than had yet appeared in English literature:

> So wondrous wild, the whole might seem
> The scenery of a fairy dream.

This passage is so well known that to quote further from it would be superfluous. Less familiar, because the poem itself has never been so much of a favourite, is the description of Coriskin in Skye in the third canto of the *Lord of the Isles*, following upon the words of Bruce:

> "A scene so rude, so wild as this,
> Yet so sublime in barrenness,
> Ne'er did my wandering footsteps press,
> Where'er I happed to roam."

No marvel thus the monarch spake;
  For rarely human eye has known
A scene so stern as that dread lake,
  With its dark ledge of barren stone.

Seems that primeval earthquakes sway
Hath rent a strange and shattered way
  Through the rude bosom of the hill,
And that each naked precipice,
Sable ravine, and dark abyss,
  Tells of the outrage still.

The wildest glen, but this, can show
Some touch of nature's genial glow;
On high Benmore green mosses grow,
And heath-bells bud in deep Glencoe,
  And copse on Cruachan Ben,
But here, above, around, below,
  On mountain, or in glen,
Nor tree, nor shrub, nor plant, nor flower,
Nor aught of vegetative power
  The weary eye may ken.
For all is rocks at random thrown,
Black waves, bare crags, and banks of stone,
  As if were here denied
The summer sun, the spring's sweet dew,
That clothe with many a varied hue
  The bleakest mountain side.
    . . . .

The evening mists, with ceaseless change,
Now clothe the mountains' lofty range,
  Now left their foreheads bare,
And round the skirts their mantle furled,
Or on the sable waters curled,

> Or, on the eddying breezes whirled,
>   Dispersed in middle air.
> And oft, condensed, at once they lower,
> When brief and fierce the mountain shower
>   Pours like a torrent down;
> And, when return the sun's glad beams,
> Whitened with foam a thousand streams
>   Leap from the mountain's crown.

A few years later, Hogg in his *Mador of the Moor* and *Queen Hynde* made the wild scenery of Scotland the background of these creations. In the introduction to the *Queen's Wake* he had already summed this up in all its aspects in the lines:

> When Mary turned her wondering eyes
> On rocks that seemed to prop the skies,
> On palace, park, and battled pile,
> On lake, on river, sea and isle,
> O'er woods and meadows bathed in dew,
> To distant mountains wild and blue,
> She thought the isle that gave her birth,
> The sweetest, wildest land on earth.

In the opening lines of *Mador* the apostrophe is more reminiscent of Scott:

> Old Caledonia! pathway of the storm
> That o'er thy wilds resistless sweeps along,
> Though clouds and snows thy sterile hills deform,
> Thou art the land of freedom and of song,
> Land of the eagle fancy, wild and strong!
> Land of the loyal heart and valiant arm!

Whatever estimates may now be put upon Hogg's poetry, it was read and admired at the time, and thus had its importance in creating a feeling for northern scenery.

Thomson had already mentioned the Hebrides more than once in his *Seasons*, in such passages as

> Where the Northern ocean, in vast whirls,
> Boils round the naked melancholy isles,
> Of farthest Thule, and the Atlantic surge
> Pours in among the stormy Hebrides.

It is instructive to compare these brief references, and the words in which they are expressed, with Scott's different treatment of the theme in the early cantos of the *Lord of the Isles*, as for example:

> Where a turret's airy head. . .
> O'er looked, dark Mull, thy mighty Sound,
> Where thwarting tides, with mingled roar,
> Part thy swarth hills from Morven's shore.
> "Daughter" she said, "these seas behold,
> Round twice a hundred islands rolled,
> From Hirt, that hears their northern roar,
> To the green Ilay's fertile shore."

In such lines the empty vastness of Thomson's "melancholy main" is replaced by something definite, which may be rugged and forbidding, but must be recognized as having a beauty of its own.

While Scott and Hogg were thus bringing the wilder scenery of Scotland before the lovers of poetry, Wordsworth was making that of the North of England a background for a number of his poems. Sometimes he describes a scene in some detail, after the manner of Scott, but more frequently it is merely indicated by a few touches, the real theme being something more abstract or intellectual. Of actual descriptions one of the fullest is that at the opening of the fifth canto of the *White Doe of Rylstone*, written at the same time as Scott's *Marmion*:

> High on a point of rugged ground,
> Among the wastes of Rylstone fell,
> Above the loftiest edge or mound
> Where foresters or shepherds dwell,
> An edifice of warlike frame
> Stands single (Norton Tower its name);
> It fronts all quarters, and looks round
> O'er path and wood, and plain and dell,
> Dark moor, and gleam of pool and stream,
> Upon a prospect without bound.

Clear as the picture is, one feels that Scott would have painted it differently, and would have made both tower and landscape take a greater hold upon the imagination.

With this development in the opening years of the nineteenth century, the scenery of the North takes a definite place in English literature, and it

is unnecessary to pursue the subject further, except
to add a few words relating to the remoter North,
which has not yet been mentioned in this connection. Here again it was Scott who led the
way in his *Pirate*, by his description of Shetland
and the Orkneys. The opening paragraphs of
that novel give pictures of Sumburgh Head, the
roost of Sumburgh, and the house of Yarlshof,
which at once introduce the reader to the wild
surroundings of a wild and, in some respects,
extravagant tale.

This beginning has not been followed up with
any great success. In spite of greatly increased
knowledge, not only of Orkney and Shetland, but
of Norway, the Færöes, and Iceland, the effect of
their scenery on English literature has been of the
slightest. There is no lack of descriptions of it in
innumerable books of travel, but of all these,
possibly the only one that lives for its literary
merit is Lord Dufferin's *Letters from High Latitudes*.
This is a surprising result, considering how greatly
the interest in these northern lands has grown
during the past century, and indicates clearly that
with regard to them the English mind has been
receptive rather than creative.

3

We have already seen that the dramatists of
the seventeenth century failed to make use of the

Northerner or the Scot as they might have been
expected to do, and that the novelists of the
eighteenth were also slow to see the possibilities
that might lie in introducing them into their
narrative. The first to make use of so obvious an
opportunity for the delineation of a special type
of character was Smollett, in his *Humphrey
Clinker*, which appeared in 1770. Lieutenant
Lismahago, who figures in the later part of that
novel, is a truly Scottish type; the various elements
of the ludicrous that appear in his character arise
from his very seriousness. He is a carefully-drawn
specimen of the argumentative Scot, whose
characteristics are excellently summed up in the
description given of him. "I think I may affirm,
that this Caledonian is a self-conceited pedant,
awkward, rude and disputatious. . .He is so
addicted to wrangling, that he will cavil at the
clearest truths, and in the pride of argumentation,
attempt to reconcile contradictions."   Smollett
evidently knew his countrymen, and the description is not yet out of date. The correctness of it,
so far as the lieutenant is concerned, is amply
illustrated in the subsequent pages of the novel.

In some respects Lieutenant Lismahago anticipates Scott's Dugald Dalgetty, in others he
comes near to Dominie Sampson. He is certainly
the only successful Scot of fiction until we come
to the Waverley novels with their marvellous

gallery of portraits from real life. To deal
adequately with these would require a volume by
itself. It is sufficient to mention only a few of
them, in the order in which Scott created them, to
show how suddenly these northern types burst
upon an admiring world, and to explain why they
took that world by storm. Scott rarely, if ever,
repeats; each new character is entirely different
from those that have preceded. There is a world
of difference between Dandy Dinmont or Dominie
Sampson in *Guy Mannering* and Jonathan Oldbuck
or Edie Ochiltree in the *Antiquary* of the same
year, or Mause or Cuddie Headrigg in *Old Mortal-
ity*. The space of two years saw the creation of
Andrew Fairservice, Baillie Nicol Jarvie, of the
Deans family and Madge Wildfire, of Caleb
Balderstone, and Dugald Dalgetty, and later on
there appear the new figures of Richie Monyplies
and Wandering Willie. This presentation of the
Scottish character is also rendered all the more
complete by the range of the Waverley novels in
point of time from the *Fair Maid of Perth* in the
fourteenth century down to *St. Ronan's Well* of the
nineteenth, and the range in space from Galloway
to the Orkneys. Few authors have covered their
own countries as extensively as Scott did his, both
in his verse and in his prose.

Skill in the portrayal of Scottish character was
fortunately not confined to Scott.   His con-

temporary, John Galt, had written the *Annals of the Parish* before *Waverley* was published, and in this, as in the *Provost* and the *Entail*, showed himself a skilful delineator of characters as different from each other as the naïve and kindly Micah Balwhidder and the shrewd, self-seeking Mr. Pawkie, although the lack of plot in such works naturally precluded them from the popularity of the Waverley novels. Scott and Galt achieved too great a triumph to be supplanted, or even rivalled, by any later writers, but ample material remained, and has existed down to the present day for such pens as those of George Macdonald, Mrs. Oliphant, and William Alexander (whose *Johnny Gibb* is unequalled of its kind), of the whole "Kailyaird School", of Robert Louis Stevenson, and others of still more recent date. A discussion of the work of these, and its place in English literature, is a subject too extensive to be dealt with here. Justice could only be done to it by a detailed study, not only of the literary art of the various writers, but of the different types of character they have endeavoured to portray, and such a study to be complete would require to be accompanied by a series of portraits of the various types, such as are to be found in the illustrated editions of *Johnny Gibb*, or Dean Ramsay's *Reminiscences*, and other works of the kind.

In this respect the North of England has been

less fortunate than Scotland, and has had no Scott or Galt to secure for it, and its typical men and women, a place in English literature. A volume of *North Country Poets* published in 1888, in which the work of fifty writers is represented, contains nothing that is really northern, except a few pieces of dialect verse. Of novels dealing with life in one or other of the northern counties, there are not a few, but probably the only one that would naturally suggest itself to the general reader is *Wuthering Heights*. The preface to the second edition of that work shows how little the success of the Scottish novel had done to bring the North of England into similar notice. That preface speaks of the general body of readers as

> Strangers . . . to whom the inhabitants, the customs, the natural characteristics of the outlying hills and hamlets in the West Riding of Yorkshire are things alien and unfamiliar.
>
> To all such, "Wuthering Heights" must appear a rude and strange production. The wild moors of the North of England can for them have no interest; the language, the manners, the very dwellings and household customs of the scattered inhabitants of those districts, must be to such readers in a great measure unintelligible, and where intelligible, repulsive.

Further on, reference is made to "the rough strong utterance, the harshly manifested passions, the unbridled aversions, and headlong partialities of unlettered moorland hinds and rugged moorland squires, who have grown up untaught and unchecked, except by mentors as harsh as themselves".

The interest in *Wuthering Heights* is centred in the persons of the story, and the bleak moorland surroundings are only a fitting background for the gloomy drama. Neither the personages nor the scenery are typical of the North of England as a whole; it is too large and too varied to be comprised in a single work. It is to be regretted that there are not a dozen more tales comparable, even if not equal, to *Wuthering Heights*, in which justice might be done to other aspects of northern life and nature. Both the past and the present could furnish as ample material for the writer as Scotland has done for the last hundred years.

4

If the northern Englishman and the Lowland Scot were so long in making their entrance upon the stage of English literature, it could not be expected that the Highlander would have any advantage over them. Even the older Scottish writers had either ignored him, or regarded him only with hostility, or as an object of ridicule. He was to them essentially a wild creature, with whom they had nothing in common. That he had some literature was known to them; they had heard of Finn mac Coul and Goll mac Morna, but the Highland or Irish bard was a person for whom they had no admiration. In the poem of the *Howlat*, the rook comes to the parliament of birds as "a bard out of Ireland, with *bannachadé*". How little respect was given to the "blessing of God", when expressed in Gaelic, may be gathered from the incident related in a fragmentary chronicle which tells how Sir Gilbert MacLean and Sir Morice MacFadyen waylaid the Bishop of Glasgow with an armed force, and spoke to him with "felloun" words and scorn, and "for dispite" saluted him in Erse, saying *bannachadee*. Dunbar's opinion of the Highlander and of Gaelic appears plainly in more than one of his poems—in the *Flyting* when he taunts Kennedy with being proficient only in "sic eloquence as they in Erschry use", in the pieces on *Sir Thomas Norray* and *Donald Owir*, and in the *Dance of the Seven Deadly Sins*, where even Mahoun himself finds the shouting of MacFadyen and his fellow Highlanders so unendurable that he "smothers them with smoke".

It is significant of a lack of close acquaintance with the Highlanders that few specific actions by individuals among them are mentioned by the older Scottish writers. One, however, related by Lindsay of Pitscottie, apparently on good authority, is too unusual to be passed over. It is the first appearance of the Highlander in a dis-

tinctly humorous light. According to this very
circumstantial tale, the Bishop of Dunkeld had
gone into England on a mission to King Richard
III, and had his business attended to on the day
before the Battle of Bosworth Field. One of his
attendants, a Macgregor, saw a chance to lay
hands on the crown of England, wrapped it in his
plaid, and nearly succeeded in escaping with it.
It was missed too soon, however; the Bishop
suspected the culprit, and the Macgregor had to
admit the theft. When questioned why he had
ventured upon so daring an act, the Highlander in
broken English gave this explanation to King
Richard:

> Sir, an it be your grace's pleasure to give me leave,
> I will show you the verity wherefore and why I took
> your crown, and thought to have had the same with
> me. Sir, ye shall understand that my mother prog-
> nosticated, when I was young and would ding my
> brothers and would crab her, she would ding me and
> said I would be hanged as the rest of my forbears had
> been before me. Therefore I thought on her sayings,
> and took her to be a true woman. Yet I thought that
> it should be for no little matter that I should die that
> death. It should not be for sheep, nor cattle, nor
> horse, nor mares, as my forbears did, to steal and be
> hanged for. But I think it a great honour to my kin
> and friends for the rich crown of England that so many
> honourable men have so lately died for, some hanged,
> some beheaded and some murdered, and some have
> fought to the death for this rich crown, which ye

offered yourself within this hour to die for, ere your
enemy Harry got it off your head. By my father's
soul, sir, give me credence, if I had it in Scotland, in
Blair in Athole, there would never one of you have
seen it, fight as fast as ye will for it.

It is satisfactory to learn that the amusement
caused by Macgregor's speech saved him from the
natural consequences of his deed.   That his action
was only what the Lowlander expected of him is
shown in a short piece by Alexander Montgomery
in which the newly-created Highlander is asked
by his Maker what he intends to do: "I will to the
Lowlands, Lord, and there steal a cow."

The part played by the Highlands in the
campaigns of Montrose and Claverhouse naturally
did nothing to endear them to the Lowlanders,
and nothing to their advantage is to be learned
about them from literary sources in the seventeenth
century. An epigram on the Earl of Argyle
repeats the old distrust:

> Now Earl of Guile and Lord forlorn thou goes,
> Quitting thy Prince to serve his Spanish foes;
> No faith in plaids, no trust in Highland trews,
> Chameleon-like they change so many hues.[1]

Even as fighters it was felt that they were falling
behind the times—a feeling expressed with some
magnanimity in the ballad-verses quoted by Scott:

[1]Sir John Scot, *The Staggering State of the Scots Statesmen* (1754).

7

> The Highlandmen are pretty men
>   For handling sword and shield,
> But yet they are but simple men
>   To stand a stricken field.
>
> The Highlandmen are pretty men
>   For target and claymore,
> But yet they are but naked men
>   To face the cannon's roar.[1]

Over against this may be set the indignation with which a Gaelic poet, Iain dubh mac Iain mhic Ailein, complains that at Dunkeld the soldiers fired from cover, instead of coming out into the open and fighting it out like men. The tactics used with such success at Killiecrankie were unavailing here.

In the eighteenth century, especially after the rising of 1715, interest began to be aroused in a part of the country characterized by modes of life so different from those of England and even of the Lowlands. The information which could be given by first-hand observers like Captain Burt partly satisfied and partly stimulated this interest, and spread a knowledge of things strange in themselves, and of the names by which they were commonly known. Terms long confined to Scotland now became familiar to the English reader. Captain Burt, for example, made his readers acquainted with the meanings of *henchman*, *gilly*,

---

[1]Scott, *Waverley*, note T.

and *bard* (as used in the Highlands), with *brogues*, and *trews*, and the *kilt*, with *second sight*, the *fiery cross*, the *lifting* of cattle, and *black mail*. Pennant also in his tours in Scotland and the Hebrides of 1769 and 1772, in addition to his accounts of Highland chiefs and reivers, gave explanations of some of these terms, together with others such as *elf-shot*, *benshi*, *coranich*, and *Beltane*. By means of these and similar works, the reading public was being prepared to a large extent for appreciation of the *Lady of the Lake* and the *Lord of the Isles*, for *Waverley* and *Rob Roy*, the *Legend of Montrose* and the *Fair Maid of Perth*, without being entirely dependent on Scott's introductions and notes for the understanding of much that formed an essential element in these works. The amount of information given in these notes is indeed remarkable, and although much of it was already accessible to the general reader, its combination with an interesting or exciting tale presented it in a new and more attractive light.

It is noteworthy that the Highlanders themselves did little to dispel the general ignorance concerning them at this date. The eighteenth century saw Scottish Gaelic poetry at its highest level in the works of Alexander Macdonald and Duncan Ban Macintyre, Dugald Buchanan and William Ross, but what they produced was as widely separated from English or Scottish literature as if

it had been of another and far-off country. Even
Macpherson's Ossianic poems did little or nothing
to bring the country of their supposed origin into
a clearer light, for Macpherson felt himself obliged
to disparage contemporary life in the Highlands in
order to enhance the glory of the misty past which
he had created.

Some, however, were beginning to make bold
claims for more favourable recognition, among the
earliest being Sir Harry Erskine in his *Highland
March* with its opening lines:

> In the garb of old Gaul, with the fire of old Rome,
> From the heath-covered mountains of Scotia we come,

and containing such others as:

> Our loud-sounding pipe bears the true martial strain;
> So do we the old Scottish valour retain.

The formation of the Highland regiments after the
'45 had, of course, much to do with this new phase
of Scottish national feeling.

Just before the appearance of *Waverley*, a new
and sympathetic view of Highland life and
character had been presented to the reading public
by Mrs. Grant of Laggan in her poem the *Highlanders*, her *Letters from the Mountains*, and her
*Essays on the Superstitions of the Highlands of
Scotland*. Though frequently diffuse and over-

loaded with general reflections, these letters and essays give an account of the Highlanders which emphasizes their many and undoubted good qualities, and explains why these had previously been unknown to the Lowlanders. A certain natural partiality underlies Mrs. Grant's encomium and her account really derives much of its truth from the greater quiet and security of the Highlands after the '45, but it is significant as the first serious attempt to bring about a better understanding of the Gael of Scotland and some appreciation of his merits and virtues.

With all this in the air, it was inevitable that Sir Walter Scott in *Waverley* should adopt to some extent the romantic view of the Highlander. It is instructive to notice how this was done in particular instances—how earlier accounts, either neutral or depreciatory, were transformed by the new spirit, and a halo of romance was thrown round figures which the original narrator regarded as very commonplace. Take, for instance, Captain Burt's account of the clan bard, whom he found dining at the chief's table, but not entertained with the best of cheer.

> After some time, the chief ordered one of them to sing me a Highland song. The bard readily obeyed; and with a hoarse voice, and in a tune of various notes, began, as I was told, one of his own lyrics, and when he had proceeded to the fourth or fifth stanza, I per-

ceived, by the names of several persons, glens, and
mountains, which I had known or heard of before that
it was an account of some clan battle. But, in his
going on, the chief (who piques himself on his school
learning) at some particular passage, bid him cease,
and cried out to me, "There's nothing like that in
Virgil or Homer." I bowed, and told him that I
believed him. This, you may believe, was very
edifying and delightful.[1]

It was clearly this account which suggested to
Scott the scene in the twentieth chapter of
Waverley:

Mac-morrough, the family bard, an aged man, immediately took the hint, and began to chant, with low
and rapid utterance, a profusion of Celtic verses, which
were received by the audience with all the applause of
enthusiasm. As he advanced in his declamation, his
ardour seemed to increase. He had at first spoken
with eyes fixed on the ground; he now cast them
around as if beseeching, and anon as if commanding
attention, and his tones rose into wild and impassioned
notes, accompanied with appropriate gestures. He
seemed to Edward, who attended to him with much
interest, to recite many proper names, to lament the
dead, to apostrophize the absent, to exhort and entreat
and animate those who were present. Waverley
thought that he even discerned his own name, and was
convinced his conjecture was right, from the eyes of
the company being at that moment turned towards
him simultaneously. The ardour of the poet appeared
to communicate itself to the audience. Their wild and

[1]Burt, *Letters from the North*, vol. II, letter xxi, p. 166.

sunburnt countenances assumed a wilder and more animated expression; all bent forward towards the reciter, many sprung up and waved their arms in ecstasy, and some laid their hands on their swords. When the song ceased there was a deep pause, while the aroused feelings of the poet and of the hearers gradually subsided into their usual channel.

A year or two before, in the *Lady of the Lake*, Scott had carried back the romance of the Highlands into a much earlier period. Here he made effective use of one custom, the Fiery Cross, which had also been fully described by Captain Burt as it still existed in the eighteenth century.

On any sudden alarm and danger or distress to the chief, he gives notice of it throughout his own clan, and to such others as are in alliance with him. This is done by sending a signal, which they call the *Fiery Cross*, being two sticks tied together transversely and burned at the ends; with this, he sends directions in writing, to signify the place of rendezvous. And when the principal person of any place has received this token, he dismisses the messenger, and sends it forward to another; and so on till all have received the intelligence. Upon the receipt of this signal, all that are near immediately leave their habitations, and repair to the place of appointment with their arms, and oatmeal for their provision. This they mingle with the water of the next river or burn they come to, when hunger calls for a supply; and often for want of a proper vessel, sup the raw mixture out of the palms of their hands.[1]

[1] *Ibid.*, letter xxiii, p. 225.

By some strange lapse of thought, a real instance of Homeric nodding, Scott makes young Angus prepare to carry the Fiery Cross by first girding on his father's dirk and broadsword, though the latter would have seriously incommoded any-one running at full speed.   Not content with that, he also furnishes him with a pole-axe "to guide and stay his footing in the tide", when he has to plunge into the River Teith.   The spectacle of Angus carrying the Fiery Cross in one hand and a pole-axe in the other, with a broadsword to impede his legs as he ran, is one which Scott could never have clearly represented to himself.

Scott, however, knew his history and the High-lands too well to present only one side of the picture.   The account of them given by Baillie Nicol Jarvie in the twenty-sixth chapter of *Rob Roy* is an excellent summary of the situation as a practical Glasgow merchant was bound to see it, and equally true to probabilities is Captain Dugald Dalgetty's despair over Highland methods of fight-ing in the *Legend of Montrose*.   Taking the good with the bad, it is no unfair or imperfect picture that the genius of Scott has painted.

In point of time, Scott was anticipated by Wordsworth in several of the pieces written during his tour in Scotland in 1803.   Among these the verses on *Rob Roy's Grave* stand out prominently as an apology for those who, only two generations before, had lived according to the "good old rule, the simple plan". They form a curious combination, Rob Roy and Wordsworth, and might well seem to belong to different eras in the history of Britain; yet Wordsworth was born only thirty-six years after Rob Roy's death.

Wordsworth's interest in the Highlands also appears in the *Excursion*, where a Highland origin is assigned to the Wanderer ("Among the hills of Athole he was born"), and in sonnets composed during his later tours in Scotland in 1831 and 1833. The change that had already taken place in a few years is expressed in one of these in terms of disillusionment:

> The Pibroch's note, discountenanced or mute,
> The Roman kilt, degraded to a toy,
> Of quaint apparel for a half-spoilt boy;
> The target mouldering like ungathered fruit,
> The smoking steam-boat eager in pursuit,
> As eagerly pursued; the umbrella spread
> To weather-fend the Celtic herdsman's head—
> All speak of manners withering to the root,
> And some old honours too, and passions high.

It was, no doubt, natural for a casual tourist to get this impression; fortunately, tourist routes are not a true index to the real nature of any country.

In spite of a promising beginning, the Highlander has not made the figure in English literature of the past century that might have been expected.

Not that books about him are lacking; they are abundant. We have histories of the Highlands in general, and of many of the Highland clans and regiments; there are numerous tours in, and descriptions of, the Highlands; there are books on clan tartans, on Highland music and literature, and many novels and tales in which the country or the people play a part. Only a few of these, however, are associated with names which appear in any general history of English literature. Thomas Campbell touched the subject in a few short pieces, of which *Lochiel's Warning* is best known, and in the longer *Pilgrim of Glencoe*, written as late as 1842, and beginning with the unfortunate line:

> The sunset sheds a horizontal smile
> O'er Highland frith and Hebridean Isle!

Three lines of this, however, are worth quoting:

> All three had that peculiar courteous grace,
> Which marks the meanest of the Highland race,
> Warm hearts that burn alike in weal and woe.

If to Campbell's pieces we add Aytoun's *Funeral March of Dundee* and *Passage of the Scot*, and, in lighter vein, Clough's *Bothy*, we have named all the verse that calls for notice in this connection. The *Bothy*, in which the modern Highlands serve as a background to an Oxford idyll, is evidence, like Wordsworth's sonnet, of the remarkable change

which had come over the Highlands in the course
of a century.

If there is little in verse, there is not much
more in prose that is really significant. Stories of
the past, like Stevenson's *Kidnapped* and *Catriona*,
or Neil Munro's *John Splendid*, however original
in plot, or excellent in the telling, are still in the
old strain of *Rob Roy* and *Waverley*, and have
hardly done more than maintain or revive an
interest in the older Highlands. The Highlander
of to-day or of the nineteenth century has only
partly been represented in the work of William
Black and Neil Munro on the one side, and that
of William Sharp on the other, and still offers a
marvellous field for any writer who could treat the
theme in its varied aspects, and do for the Scottish
Gael what Scott and others have done for the
Lowlander. There is, perhaps, more hope for this,
now that plays and novels are actually being
written in Gaelic, and writers in that language are
animated by literary ideals which until now have
been quite foreign to it.

5

Still less than the Highlander did the contemporary Orcadian or Shetlander, the Norwegian
or Icelander, come within the literary horizon of
the seventeenth and eighteenth centuries. Not
that contact with the Scandinavian countries was

altogether lacking, but the English and Scottish merchants who brought timber from Norway, and stock-fish from Iceland, were not interested in these countries except for purely practical reasons. For literary contacts there was, indeed, little opportunity, for the modern literature of Norway, like that of Denmark and Sweden, was only beginning in the seventeenth century. Curiously enough the first Norwegian poet of note, Peder Dass, and the first Danish, Thomas Kingo, were the sons of Scottish parents, a fact which may not be altogether accidental.

Though various accounts of Orkney and Shetland had appeared in print before 1800, it is again to the genius of Scott that we owe the first literary presentation of Shetland life in the *Pirate*, partly corresponding to fact, but largely blended with imaginative echoes of the past. The story itself is not one of his best, and the character of Norna is too fanciful, but the *Pirate* gives a remarkable amount of information regarding Shetland and its inhabitants, their customs and their speech, all of which must have been quite new to almost every reader. If Scott did not attain his best level in this instance, no one has done better since; the *Pirate* has had no notable successor, although much has been written during the past hundred years from which a less imaginative idea of life in the northern islands may be derived.

Still later in the nineteenth century, with increasing knowledge of Norway, English writers begin to use that country as the scene, in whole or in part, of works of fiction, none of which have taken any prominent place in English literature. Harriet Martineau's *Feats on the Fjord*, Catherine Ray's *Farm on the Fjord*, or Edna Lyall's *Hardy Norseman*, and similar works, do demonstrate that Norway interested the writers, and the reading of them has undoubtedly brought Norway into wider notice, but something more than a brief visit to any country is necessary before even a great writer can successfully catch or reproduce the spirit of it. The same remark may without much injustice be applied to the few novels of which the scene is laid in Iceland, as the *Bondman* and the *Prodigal Son*. Much more important, from every point of view, are the numerous translations of Norwegian writers which have been made during the past fifty years— translations from the works of Bjørnson, Ibsen, Lie, Boyesen, Hamsun, *etc*. The extent to which such translations are steadily being produced and widely read is a proof that there is a lively interest in the North, which will be prompt to respond to any writer who can do it justice.[1]

---

[1]A good survey of the growth of this interest is given by C. B. Burchardt in *English Views on Norwegian Life and Literature* (1920).

Lecture IV

THE growth of interest in the North coincided with the beginnings of romanticism in England, and was an important (though not the only) factor in that movement. An interest in what was regarded as "Gothic" and "Romantic" very readily included northern themes within its scope, and these probably helped in no small degree to free the movement from the formalism which marks it at the outset. The break with classicism was not an abrupt one; it was at the outset more a change in matter than in form. The literary ballad, for example, differed as much from the genuine ballad as it did from the classical verse against which it was a reaction. Romanticism, however, had barely established itself as a new tendency in English literature when it was strengthened by the simultaneous influence of Celtic and old Norse poetry. The first of these was not absolutely genuine, and the second was largely misunderstood, but there was enough that was real and new in both to bring the North into a literary prominence which it had never enjoyed before. The Celtic, in Macpherson's *Ossian*, had slightly the start of the Norse, and obtained a more rapid, and at the time a far greater, success. It succeeded, not so much because it was northern, but because it was new both in matter and in form. The latter was almost an accident. Macpherson had hesitated between the conventional rhymed couplet and the prose to which he owed much of his success.

It is unnecessary to enter into the full story of Macpherson's *Ossian*.[1] The points of importance are these. Beginning with loose renderings of some of the genuine Ossianic ballads, Macpherson almost at once entered upon the career of invention which produced *Fingal* and *Temora* and the score of minor pieces which are so difficult to distinguish from each other—*Cath-Loda, Carthon, Oina-morul, Calthon and Colmal, etc.* In addition to the poems, he conveyed to his readers, in notes and dissertations, a marvellous amount of doubtful or spurious information regarding Celtic poetry, and the early Celtic period. There were, of course, many who disbelieved in the genuineness of *Ossian*; that there were so many who accepted it is striking evidence of the ignorance concerning the North and its history, its language and literature, that prevailed at the time. Even the incongruity of the state of

[1]A good account may be found in J. S. Smart's *James Macpherson, An Episode in Literature* (1905). The extensive literature on the subject is covered in *Macpherson's Ossian and the Ossianic Controversy: A contribution towards a bibliography*, by George F. Black (New York Public Library, 1926).

culture in Ossianic days was not enough to arouse suspicion in the believers. Taking it as Macpherson had devised it, they merely contrasted it with the barbarism which they supposed, on imperfect evidence, to have prevailed in Scandinavia at the same period. Dr. Hugh Blair, the unsuspecting apostle of Macpherson, expressly draws the contrast. Citing the *Death-song of Ragnar Lodbrog*, he says: "This is such poetry as we might expect from a barbarous nation. It breathes a most ferocious spirit. It is wild, harsh, and irregular." (All this, naturally, in ignorance of the fact that the famous *Death-song* is a late and highly artificial composition.)

> But when we open the works of Ossian, a very different scene presents itself. There we find the fire and the enthusiasm of the most early times, combined with an amazing degree of regularity and art. We find tenderness and even delicacy of sentiment, greatly predominant over fierceness and barbarity. . .When we turn from the poetry of Lodbrog to that of Ossian, it is like passing from a savage desert into a fertile and cultivated country.

In keeping with this contrast, it is worthy of note that nowhere does Blair make any allusion to any northern elements in *Ossian*.

Considering the success of Macpherson, it is rather surprising that the similar attempt of Dr. John Smith in his *Galic Antiquities* to manufacture "poems of Ossian, Ullin and other bards" should have failed to attract attention, especially as in his later *Sean Dana* he anticipated Macpherson in providing a Gaelic text to accompany the English. More notable, however, is the lack of interest in such of the genuine Ossianic ballads as were printed while the controversy was going on, *e.g.*, by Thomas Hill in the *Gentleman's Magazine* or by Miss Brookes in her *Reliques of Irish Poetry*. Macpherson had, of course, carefully created a prejudice against these beforehand by denouncing the bards and all their works, in more than one passage, as being representative of "the wildest regions of fiction and romance". The impression thus created, added to ignorance of Gaelic, unfortunately prevented the ballads from taking the place they might have had in the romantic movement. Even Jerome Stone's rendering of the *Lay of Fraoch* evidently failed to excite curiosity regarding the literature to which it belonged.

The truth seems to be that it was difficult, if not impossible, for eighteenth-century readers to appreciate northern material in its genuine form; it had to be modified to suit a taste which was changing, but had not changed sufficiently to admire what was entirely new and unfamiliar. Scholars might be attracted by the old Norse and Icelandic poetry in its original form, or even in Latin translations, and might venture, like Hickes and Percy, to produce plain prose versions of it,

8

but anyone who attempted to render it in verse felt it necessary to make it conform to the taste of the day by introducing epithets and phrases entirely lacking in the original. Thomas Warton, the elder, the pioneer in this line, affords as good an example of the method as any, in his rendering of the last verse of Ragnar's *Death-song*. The original runs: "The Goddesses, whom Odin has sent to me from his hall, invite me home. Gladly shall I drink ale with the Gods in the high-seat. The hours of life are past; laughing I shall die." The old Icelandic text of this is deliberately composed in a simple metre and direct language to give an impression of antiquity. Now observe how the eighteenth century speaks in Warton's lines:

> Hark! how the solemn Sisters call,
> And point aloft to Odin's hall!
> I come, I come, prepare full bowls,
> Fit banquet for heroic Souls.
> What's Life?—I scorn this idle breath,
> I smile in the embrace of Death.

Warton's verses have remained in obscurity while Gray's *Fatal Sisters* and *Descent of Odin*, published twenty years later, have been familiar to several generations of readers. The method of translation is the same; the original is so amplified that the additions are often the most significant part of a line, and it is precisely in virtue of these that the

piece is accepted and admired as good poetry.
One verse in the original of the *Descent of Odin*
runs thus: "Rind bears Váli in Western halls,
When one night old Váli will slay him. He
neither washes his hands, nor combs his hair, till
he sends to death the slayer of Balder. Unwilling
have I spoken; now I shall be silent." It is out of
this that Gray has produced these lines:

> In the caverns of the West,
> By Odin's fierce embrace compressed,
> A wondrous boy shall Rinda bear,
> Who ne'er shall comb his raven hair,
> Nor wash his visage in the stream,
> Nor see the sun's departing beam,
> Till he on Hoder's corse shall smile
> Flaming on the funeral pile.
> Now my weary lips I close;
> Leave me, leave me, to repose.

What is true of Warton and Gray is equally
true of their successors, of Mathias, of Cottle, of
Herbert, and others, few of whom are better in
this respect, while some are worse. Even in
William Morris's *Sigurd the Volsung*, the same
device appears, though with more justification in
an original poem, when he takes over from the
saga the brief verses with which the newly-
awakened Brynhild addresses the Day and the
Night, the Gods and Goddesses, and the Earth.

> All hail, O Day, and thy Sons, *and thy kin of coloured
>   things,*

Hail, *following* Night, and thy Daughter, *that leadeth
    thy wavering wings,*
Look down with unangry eyes on us *to-day alive,*
And give us *the hearts* victorious, *and the gain for which
    we strive.*
All hail, ye "Lords" of *God-home,* and ye "Queens"
    of the House of Gold
Hail thou *dear* Earth *that hearest, and thou Wealth of
    field and fold.*
Give us, your noble children, *the glory of* wisdom and
    speech,
And *the hearts and* the hands of healing, *and the mouths
    and the hands that teach.*[1]

These are noble lines, and they are undoubtedly
in the spirit of the original, but the chances are
that the very phrases which will make the deepest
impression on the reader are those which character-
ize the poetry of Morris, and are not even suggested by anything in the original.

This mode of translation has a natural origin
in the difficulty of doing anything else. Neither
the simple form of the *Edda* poems, nor the
complicated structure of Scaldic verse, can readily
be transmuted into English poetry; it is necessary
to add to the one, and to make the other intelligible
without simplifying too much the never-failing
precision and elaborateness of the metre. In this
respect it is more difficult to translate old Icelandic
than Gaelic poetry, for the latter, although it has

[1]The italicized portions are Morris's own additions.

the complexity of rhyme, is more diffuse, and is free from the artificial poetic diction cultivated by the Scalds. Hence there is little alternative for the translator, unless he is willing to take a world of pains to produce a result, the skill of which the English reader would probably fail to appreciate.

Original poems in English on Scandinavian themes have not been particularly successful. Scott's *Harold the Dauntless* is usually omitted without explanation or apology from editions of his poetical works, and there can be few of this generation who have read Hogg's *Queen Hynde* or Tennant's *Thane of Fife*. More success has attended the re-telling in verse of themes from the *Edda* or the sagas—Matthew Arnold's *Balder Dead*, or William Morris's *Lovers of Gudrun, Fostering of Aslaug*, and *Sigurd the Volsung*. Of these, the last-named is the best, because the long, swinging line carries on with sufficient vigour a tale replete with incident. The *Lovers of Gudrun* suffers both from slowness of movement and from having to bear comparison with its original, a saga which ranks among the best achievements of old Icelandic literature. A different mode of treating the original source is seen in Longfellow's *Saga of King Olaf*, which was clearly suggested by the Swedish poet Tegner's version of the *Frithjof Saga*. The extent to which this method of rendering an old tale excited admiration is shown by the remarkable number of times the Swedish poem has been translated into English. Longfellow himself rendered passages from it. It has no doubt helped to maintain the popular misconception (in which even Longfellow seems to have shared) that a saga is a poem.

Old Icelandic prose has been more copiously and more successfully translated than the poetry, and there is no saga of first-rate importance that cannot be read in at least one English version. The writing of good saga-prose is, however, almost as difficult in English as the proper rendering of Scaldic verse, and the reader may well feel at a loss among the widely different styles that have been adopted by different translators. Beyond translating, little use has been made in English of this great northern literature. Carlyle in his first lecture on *Heroes and Hero-worship*, and his *Early Kings of Norway*, stands almost alone in this respect. In both of these, the choice of a northern subject by a great writer is more remarkable than the actual treatment of it. The account of Scandinavian mythology is mainly an attempt, looking at it from the outside and without clear knowledge of its history or background, to find a deep meaning in the myths, and to make out that in strength and sincerity they are superior to those of ancient Greece. The *Early Kings* are hardly more than a summary of Snorri's *Heimskringla* for young readers, with a Carlylean touch here and there in the re-telling.

2

We are now in a position to form some estimate of the place which the North really holds in English literature. We have seen that much has been written about it during the past century and a half, and that if we use the term "literature" in its widest sense, that of the North would fill a library by itself—and a most interesting collection of books the shelves of that library would contain. Perhaps such a collection ought to be brought together, to serve as a centre for northern studies, out of which might come some fresh inspiration, some new movement like that which first brought northern themes into English literature in the days of Gray and Percy.

If we limit the application of the term, however, to those works which would naturally and inevitably be mentioned in any history of English letters, we find that the names of authors entitled to notice on this ground shrink at once to a small number, and that in most cases what they have written concerning the North forms but a minor portion of their work. It is useless, as we have seen, to begin this survey at an earlier date than the middle of the eighteenth century, and it is significant that even after that date the special studies that have been made of some aspects of the subject have to fetch much of their material from the by-ways of literature, from books long forgotten, from articles and verses never reprinted from the magazines in which they appeared. Consequently there are not so many names to be considered, and a survey of them can be briefly made.

The first that naturally fall to be mentioned are Collins, Gray, and Percy. From Collins we have but the one ode on the *Superstitions of the Highlands*, written in 1749, but not printed till 1788. Gray, like Collins, was not a prolific poet, and his two northern pieces occupy but a few pages of his collected poems. It is the name of Gray, and the date at which they appeared, that gives them their importance. Percy holds his place in literary history by his *Reliques*, in which the North has only a modest place; his five *Runic Pieces* and his translation of Mallet's *Northern Antiquities* would not by themselves have made him famous, however much they may have served to rouse interest in others.

From the Lake school of poets, with their new views on poetry, something might have been expected—some inspiration from that northern scenery which was beginning to be admired, from the rugged northern character which had not yet been properly recognized. Coleridge and Southey,

however, remain practically untouched by the new
influence; it is only in Wordsworth that it is
reflected to an extent which permeated much of
his poetry.   Yet even Wordsworth is not primarily
a poet of the North; his interests are in the main
introspective; he has not the pure physical delight
in landscape that appears in Scott, nor is he
interested in the hill-folk as such, but only as they
present matter for narrative or reflective verse.
Hence, if one were to attempt to distinguish in his
poetry between that portion which springs from
northern sources and that which is unconnected
with these, the latter would be found to be far in
excess of the former.   This is not at all surprising;
it merely emphasizes the fact that the best literature has found it difficult to make free use of
northern material, even when the writer lived in
the midst of it and was in sympathy with it.

Of Scott it might seem unnecessary to speak in
this connection, when so much of his work has
already been drawn upon by way of illustration.
Even Scott, however, did not by any means limit
his interests to the North—witness the series of
novels relating to English and French history, and
to the Crusades, his *Life of Napoleon*, his *Life and
Works of Swift*, in nineteen volumes, *etc*.   Galt,
too, was a prolific writer on many themes; of
forty-four titles with which his name is connected
less than half are on Scottish subjects.   In this

9

respect both Scott and Galt differ from James Hogg, whose themes, in verse and prose, are consistently Scottish, although a Scottish strain is not always prominent in the treatment.

How slight the Scottish element is in the work of Campbell has already been indicated. The situation is well summed up by one of his editors: "Campbell drew imagery from Scottish scenery, and he has let slip a few provincialisms, but on the whole, his muse, instead of displaying a Scottish nationality, puts it aside as far as she can."[1]

Aytoun, whose *Lays of the Scottish Cavaliers* and *Bothwell* are the best successors to the poetry of Scott, had other interests which occupy a much larger space in his collected verse. It is, however, by these pieces that he holds his place in literature, not by his *Poland* or *Homer*, his translations from Goethe and other sources, or his drama of *Firmilian*.

It is needless to emphasize the comparative slightness of the northern interest in the work of Matthew Arnold and of Carlyle, whose writings would lose but little if all that belongs to this theme were eliminated. Even William Morris, one may safely say, has been more widely read for other things than for the *Lovers of Gudrun* or *Sigurd the Volsung*.

Taken comparatively in this way, the record

[1] W. Allingham in the Aldine edition of Campbell's *Poems*, p. xxvi

is not a striking one, however much may be made of it if it is considered by itself in all its details. It is obvious that much is lacking which forms a natural part of any great literature. There is a fair quantity of lyric and narrative poetry of high merit, but there is no epic except that of Morris, directly based on the *Völsunga Saga*, although the past history of the North, whether of Britain or of Scandinavia, could supply numerous subjects for epic poetry. In the drama, *Macbeth* and *Hamlet* remain the only great plays made from northern material. One cannot say that Scotland is adequately represented by the *Gentle Shepherd*, still less by *Douglas*, the *Regicide*, *Halidon Hill*, the *Doom of Devorgoil*, or Tennant's long forgotten *Cardinal Beaton* and *John Balliol*, nor is it likely that Burns would have been more successful if he had written his intended "Bruce". That no English dramatist of note since Shakespeare should have selected a northern subject is, however, surprising, for here again there is no lack of material, either for the historical play or for tragedy. Swinburne's triology of *Chastelard*, *Bothwell*, and *Mary Stuart* thus remains the only modern attempt by a great English poet to present a Scottish theme in dramatic form.

So far as themes from the North of England or Scotland are concerned, we must recognize the fact that the deficiency lies in the absence of great writers capable of hearing the voice of the North, and giving expression to its suggestions. That the reading public will readily respond to the call is shown by the success of those who have already voiced it in the past: no Burns or Hogg, no Scott or Galt will ever lack a hearing because they speak of northern things. This is equally true of those who have drawn their inspiration from Celtic or Scandinavian antiquity, although their task has been a more difficult one to do well. It is difficult not only because the themes and their legendary and historical background are unfamiliar in comparison with those of classical, romantic, or even oriental origin. That difficulty would disappear if the authors had the skill to make the new matter interesting in itself. The greatest obstacle lies in the lack of familiar English words to express some of the fundamental terms which occur in the older literature of the North, such as *godi* or *thing* in the Icelandic sagas. The names also of persons and places are a real difficulty. A long literary tradition has made familiar the names of Greek and Roman gods and heroes, and historical persons, and of the geography of the ancient world. For Celtic and Scandinavian names there is no such tradition, and the writer is constantly forced to a choice between something correct, but uncouth or unpronounceable to English eyes, and some altered form which may equally fail to satisfy the reader.

Macpherson had no scruples in dealing boldly with names that were too Gaelic in form: *Cuchulainn, Conlaoch, Deirdre,* and *Teamhair* were transformed into *Cuthullin, Conlath, Darthula,* and *Temora*; even *Fionn* and *Goll* were improved into *Fingal* and *Gaul.* Gray and others could use Latinized forms of old Norse names like *Valhalla, Sangrida, Hela, Haco.* This is more than the modern can venture upon, and the difficulty that can be caused by a simple Icelandic name like *Gudrûn* is shown by Morris using it to rhyme with *spun* and *one.* Icelandic place-names, like *Svínadalr, Borgarfjördr, Hjardarholt,* and *Laugar,* cannot be transplanted in these forms into English verse or prose, but they do not become more poetic when translated as *Swinedale, Burgfirth, Herdholt,* and *Bathstead.* These difficulties, slight as they may seem, are really a greater bar to the re-telling of old northern or Celtic tales than the impossibility of reproducing exactly the metres of the old poetry. Compensation for the latter might be made in other ways, but the names are an integral part of the story; they cannot be eliminated, and they must not be altered beyond recognition. Hence, the greater success of a poem like *Sigurd,* in which the setting is less local, less restricted to actual places which cannot be altered or omitted, while the story itself, originating in Central Europe, has more in common with the usual types of mediæval romances.

These difficulties are real, but they are not insuperable. They will not deter any great writer from choosing a northern subject if it really interests him, nor prevent him from treating it with success. Anyone who essays the task at all will at least have one great advantage over his fore-runners of a century ago—he has ample means of ascertaining what the early life and early litera-ture of the North really was, of seeing them without illusion and without prejudice, and realizing that neither the barbaric nor the romantic (as the eighteenth century understood the term) has any place in them. It would be impossible now for anyone to assert, as Macpherson did, evidently with little fear of contradiction, that the following lines were "the beginning of a poem, translated from the Norse into the Gaelic language, and from the latter transferred into English".

> When Harold, with golden hair, spread o'er Lochlin his high commands; where with justice he ruled the tribes, who sunk, subdued beneath his sword; abrupt rises Gormal in snow! The tempests roll dark on his sides, but calm above, his vast forehead appears. White-issuing from the skirts of his storms, the troubled torrents pour down his sides. . . .

Scott knew far more about old Norse and Icelandic poetry than Macpherson, and knowledge of the subject had become more general between 1773 and 1821, but in the *Pirate* he is quite as regardless of accuracy in this respect as the author of *Ossian*. One ought not, perhaps, to blame a romancer for taking liberties with the truth, but erroneous ideas with regard to the nature of old Scandinavian poetry could only be perpetuated by Scott's inventions. Norna, he tells his readers,

> chanted a Norwegian invocation, still preserved in the Island of Uist [*sic*], under the name of the Song of the Reim-kennar [a compound of Scott's own making] though some call it the Song of the Tempest. The following is a free translation, it being impossible to render literally many of the elliptical and metaphorical terms of expression peculiar to the ancient Northern poetry.

Part of one stanza will suffice as an example of what "the ancient Northern poetry" never even remotely resembled:

> Stern eagle of the far north-west,
> Thou that bearest in thy grasp the thunder-bolt,
> Thou whose rustling pinions stir the ocean to madness,
> Thou the destroyer of herds, thou the scatterer of navies.
> Though thy scream be as loud as the cry of a perishing nation,
> Though the rushing of thy wings be like the roaring of ten thousand waves.
> Yet, hear, in thine ire and thy haste,
> Hear thou the voice of the Reim-kennar.

Similarly, in a later chapter, the "bard" Halcro, several of whose pieces were "translations or

imitations from the Scaldic sagas", is made to
chant "the following imitation of a northern war-
song", which is equally unlike anything conceived
by any Scald.

> The sun is rising dimly red,
> The wind is wailing low and dread,
> From his cliff the eagle sallies,
> Leaves the wolf his darksome valleys. . . .

Setting aside the method of pure invention, as well
as artificial translations after the manner of Gray,
there is still ample scope for the poet in old
northern themes, re-telling them for modern times
without losing the spirit of those in which they
were created. This has already been done in
various ways; by Arnold and Morris in poems in
which the metre is uniform throughout; by Longfellow in his *Saga of King Olaf* in a succession of
pieces in different metres. This is the method of
Tegner in his *Frithjof's Saga*, and of the Danish
poet, Valdemar Rørdam, in his *Beovulf*, while in a
more elaborate form it has been practised for over
five centuries by the Icelanders in their *Rímur*.
The complex metre of these it would be hopeless
to imitate, but the variety given by a series of
different verse-forms is of great value, not only
in maintaining the interest of the reader, but in
enabling the author to vary the form according
to the turns of the tale.

In one instance the form of northern poetry has been successfully carried over into English. Longfellow's acquaintance with the Finnish *Kalevala* supplied him with the metre of his *Hiawatha*, and with the metre followed inevitably the repetitional style of Finnish poetry. It may be doubted whether the legends of the American Indian would ever have attained so much popularity in any other form.

It is difficult, even for the most acute observer, to say whither literary movements are tending at any particular time, and to foretell what the next few years will bring forth. Who, in the early years of the nineteenth century, even looking back on the forty or fifty years during which romanticism had been steadily growing, could have foreseen the rapid development which was about to take place? It is easy, at a later date, to trace the causes that have produced a group of writers at any time, but there is nothing to ensure that such a group will arise, nor anything to justify us in supposing that a particular movement has spent itself. If, however, we try to conjecture what part the North may play in English literature of the future, there are several things which make it probable that it will not be unimportant. I have already mentioned the greatly increased interest in northern literature, manifested by the number of translations and other works that appeal to the general reader and are widely circulated and read. A counterpart to this is the intense interest which the Scandinavian countries have in English literature and the English-speaking world — an interest greatly strengthened by the number of settlers from these countries on this side of the Atlantic. When Canadian Icelanders can successfully translate the poetry of their own country into English, and English poetry into Icelandic, it is obvious that two things are coming together which formerly lay wide apart, and no one can foretell what may come of the union.

Another important factor is that the old North, instead of being the outermost bounds of civilization and culture, is steadily having that limit pushed to a higher latitude. Partly by ease of communication, partly by the extension of commercial enterprise to areas beyond them, Norway and Iceland have come nearer to the rest of Europe in recent years. In Canada and Alaska a new North is being created undreamt of fifty years ago, and in the search for new routes between the Old World and the New, even Greenland is acquiring a new interest. This new North has already made itself heard in literature; there is every likelihood that its voice will grow clearer and stronger with time. Under these new conditions, with all these new possibilities, it may at any time evolve a fresh type of literature which will affect the rest of the world. Twice or thrice already the North has done this. The poems of Ossian had almost a greater vogue and a more powerful influence on the continent of Europe than in the country of their origin. They were read and quoted, translated and imitated, admired and extravagantly praised, in almost every country of Europe, and remained in favour in some of these after they had almost ceased to be read at home. Their influence went not only south and east, but also northwards; portions of them were being translated into Icelandic almost a century after they first appeared.

Another instance of the northern influence in Europe is that of the historical novel. Although fore-runners of this appear in England during the last thirty years of the eighteenth century, and Jane Porter anticipated Scott with *Thaddeus of Warsaw* in 1803, and the *Scottish Chiefs* in 1809, it was the author of *Waverley* who at last set the model by his marvellous series of romances based on historic persons and incidents. Before long the model was being followed by almost every country in Europe, and, while few of these have produced anything equally original or of the same literary worth, the literature of several nations would be distinctly poorer if all that was written under this influence were to be withdrawn from it. Considering the vogue which both American and English literature have in other countries at the present day, there can be little doubt that any new impulse from the North would meet with a quick response. The influence of Ibsen on the modern stage is a proof that any new development would not long remain unnoticed and untried.

There are other movements, too new as yet for their exact significance to be estimated, which point in the same direction. On both sides of the Highland line in Scotland there is fresh literary activity on a basis of national feeling and national speech. Conscious efforts of this kind are apt to be of mediocre value in their early stages, but they can improve with surprising rapidity. There is a world of difference between what was written in Norway in the early days of the Norwegian revival and what has been written since. The same is true of Friesland, and it is worthy of note that the younger school of Frisian writers is keenly interested in the North, and is consciously striving to combine that interest with the study of English and its literature, and to assimilate what it finds best in both.

The question may properly be asked: What is there in the older North, whether Scottish or Scandinavian, which could be used by writers of the present day? With what subjects could it supply them out of which something worth having could be made either in prose or verse?

The answer to that is that the great store of northern lore has yet barely been touched by good English writers. The early history of Scotland, whether Lowland or Highland, is represented only by *Macbeth*; yet it is a period in which, for centuries, stirring movements of races were taking place, a series of scenes in which Picts and Scots, Angles and Norsemen, Welsh and Irish play their parts, and out of which now and then an event or a person stands out clearly through the haze of antiquity. Much research has gone to the clearing up of this early period; it is not difficult to learn all that can be known with certainty about it, but no one has as yet sought to present any part of it as a great writer could present it in one form or another. The accumulation of bare historical facts, with ingenious conjectures to fill the gaps, does not make the story a living one; that can only be done with the help both of historical insight and poetic imagination, and no one has yet ventured to undertake any part of the task.

In the Scandinavian North there is even more opportunity for accomplishing great things, since the old northern literature itself has preserved so much knowledge of the past, and has set so high a standard for the telling of it. The ancient mythology and religion are accessible to everyone in the various translations of the *Edda* poems and Snorri's *Edda*, and in special works in the subject.

The sagas of the kings of Norway and Denmark, of famous Icelanders, of the Færöes and the Orkneys, of legendary or fictitious heroes of antiquity, have been translated in abundance. In all of those there is untold material for writers to work upon—material which could be so selected or modified as to avoid the difficulties already spoken of. There are abundant themes for lyric or narrative poetry, for the drama, for historical fiction, and for pure history, of which surprisingly little use has yet been made. These themes only require to be worthily handled to be favourably received, to arouse interest in the sources from which they come, and to draw attention to the inexhaustible North which has so long waited for its day to come.

Even the forms of northern poetry may yet be studied with advantage by English poets. To reproduce to any extent the rich vocalization of Gaelic poetry would add a new quality to English verse, and give fuller opportunity for close harmony of sound and sense. The strict alliteration and complicated rhyming of Icelandic poetry would be a hard thing, if not impossible, to imitate exactly, but some approximation to it would at times be a more fitting medium for northern themes than any of the ordinary forms of English verse. A careful study of the rules of Icelandic metre would show how inartistic and unsatisfactory are the attempts that have been made to write alliterative verse in modern English, and might serve to show the way to something better. This, however, is speculative, and even with the accepted forms of English verse there is an ample field in the old northern past for the poet who will again address himself to the *Harp of the North* in such lines as those of Scott:

> O, wake once more! how rude so e'er the hand
> That ventures o'er thy magic maze to stray;
> O, wake once more! though scarce my skill command
> Some feeble echoing of thine earlier lay;
> Though harsh and faint, and soon to die away,
> And all unworthy of thy nobler strain,
> Yet if one heart throb higher at its sway,
> The wizard note has not been touched in vain.
> Then silent be no more!   Enchantress, wake again!

Lightning Source UK Ltd.
Milton Keynes UK
UKHW012358200722
406167UK00001B/319